THE POCKET GUIDE

TO THE

AFTERLIFE

D1018212

Published by Bloomsbury USA, New York

All papers used by Bloomsbury USA are natural, recyclable products made from wood grown in well-managed forests. The manufacturing processes conform to the environmental regulations of the country of origin.

LIBRARY OF CONGRESS CATALOGING-IN-PUBLICATION DATA HAS BEEN APPLIED FOR.

ISBN-10 1-59691-584-6
ISBN-13 978-1-59691-584-8

Illustrations: Ryan Hobson
Design: Paul Barrett
Editorial: Kristin Mehus-Roe
Production: Shirley Woo

First U.S. Edition 2009

1 3 5 7 9 10 8 6 4 2

Produced by becker&mayer! Book Producers.
Manufactured in Singapore.

THE POCKET GUIDE

→ TO THE ←

AFTERLIFE

91 PLACES DEATH MIGHT TAKE YOU

by AUGUSTA MOORE and ELIZABETH RIPLEY

BLOOMSBURY

Contents

5	Introduction
6	Ásatrú
10	Atheism
14	Baha'i Faith
16	Buddhism
20	The Church of Christ, Scientist
24	The Church of Jesus Christ of Latter-Day Saints
28	The Church of Satan
30	Confucianism
34	Druze Faith
38	Eckankar
42	Gnosticism
46	Greek Orthodox
50	Hinduism
54	International Society for Krishna Consciousness
58	Islam
62	Jainism
66	Jehovah's Witnesses
70	Judaism
74	Kabbalah
76	Lutheranism
80	Modern Druidism
84	Nation of Islam
88	Rastafari Movement
92	Roman Catholicism
96	The Rosicrucian Fellowship
100	Santeria
104	Scientology
108	Seventh-Day Adventist
112	Shakers
116	Shinto
120	Sikhism
124	Snake-handling Pentacostalism
128	Spiritualism
132	The Twelve Tribes
136	The Unification Church
140	Universal Sufism
144	Vodou
148	Wicca
152	Yazdânism
156	Zoroastrianism
160	About the Authors

Introduction

What do a Zoroastrian fire priest, a snake-handling Pentecostal, and a member of the Greek Orthodox Church all have in common? More than you might think. In fact, followers of each of these religions, literally poles apart and wildly different culturally and ethnically, have somewhere along the way found a guiding force and a sense of cosmic order in religious tenets, rituals, traditions, and some promise of eternal reward. In fact, though a total of forty religions are explored in this book, we think you might be surprised at how many similarities exist between them. Sure, many religions, like strict parents, espouse the notion that you have only one chance to get it right before meeting your fate in a form of paradisaical heaven or a fiery hell, while others allow their followers a second chance, usually in the form of additional lives, to learn from their mistakes. Yet, fundamentally, all of these faiths are rooted in the notion that you can rise up and attain the good life (and a desirable afterlife), be it through tithing, ancestor worship, limiting your sybaritic pursuits, or taking a few turns on the reincarnation wheel. Not so far off from the quintessential American Dream, when you think of it; the possibility for redemption waits around every corner; some blocks are just a lot longer than others.

And while some of us keep the faith of our parents and their parents before them, for some people religious choice is like perusing a mail-order catalog, glossy pages spread out before them: Join the Catholics at Sunday mass or meditate on the Noble Eightfold Path as a Buddhist. Or, perhaps, celebrating the summer solstice as a Modern Druid is more your speed? (If you're not sure, signing up for the free Scientology personality test might help you narrow it down.)

If you're lucky, you probably have about seventy-seven years to spend on this planet, while the hereafter would appear to last a good bit longer. So, before you decide to spend your mortal turn practicing Kabbalah or becoming a distance-learning Rosicrucian, it makes good sense to factor in how you might spend eternity. So, do yourself a favor—enlighten yourself.

How to use this book:

= Death

= Follow here!

Ásatrú

Not a religion for the faint of heart, this modern manifestation of ancient Norse paganism was resurrected in the late nineteenth century and granted official religious status in Iceland in 1972. It has since been on a rapid rise in northern Europe, as well as in the United States. In keeping with modern sensibilities, devotees of Ásatrú follow Norse mythology to varying degrees, from quite literal to more symbolic interpretations. All Ásatrúan doctrine, however, is rooted in the adventures of a rowdy and quarrelsome host of gods and goddesses—Thor, Odin, Frigg, and Hel among them—whose favorite pastime seems to be pummeling one another. In true Viking spirit, these deities prize military valor and richly reward those mortals who die honorably in combat. In fact, this religion makes a great Army recruiting device; if you don't die in battle, you're not going to have a fun afterlife.

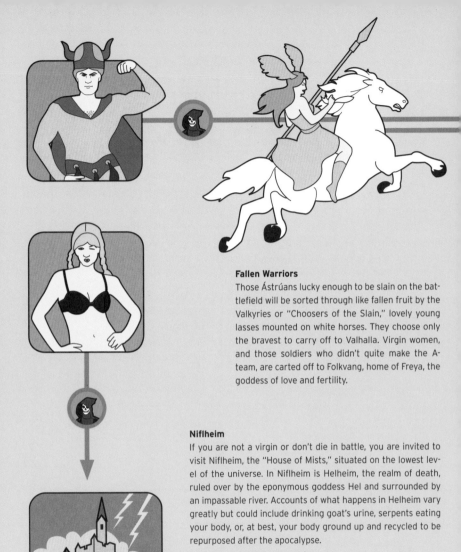

Fallen Warriors

Those Ástrúans lucky enough to be slain on the battlefield will be sorted through like fallen fruit by the Valkyries or "Choosers of the Slain," lovely young lasses mounted on white horses. They choose only the bravest to carry off to Valhalla. Virgin women, and those soldiers who didn't quite make the A-team, are carted off to Folkvang, home of Freya, the goddess of love and fertility.

Niflheim

If you are not a virgin or don't die in battle, you are invited to visit Niflheim, the "House of Mists," situated on the lowest level of the universe. In Niflheim is Helheim, the realm of death, ruled over by the eponymous goddess Hel and surrounded by an impassable river. Accounts of what happens in Helheim vary greatly but could include drinking goat's urine, serpents eating your body, or, at best, your body ground up and recycled to be repurposed after the apocalypse.

Valhalla

Valhalla, or the "Hall of the Slain," is Odin's hall. Sort of a haven for the baddest blonds, Valhalla features 540 doors, each large enough for 800 warriors to march through shoulder to shoulder. You will feast upon Saehrimnir, a most unfortunate pig slaughtered and resurrected *daily* by the cook of the gods (clearly not a porcine-friendly religion). In Valhalla, the Valkyries morph into tough serving wenches, in charge of topping off your vessel with mead. All this while you await the battle of all battles, Ragnarök. Then it's off to war again. You'd think it would be enough to die once.

Folkvang

If the Valkyries don't think you're up to Odin's speed, then it's off to the beautiful palace Folkvang and Freya's hall, Sessrumnir. Here, love songs play continually—one can only hope they're a little more Al Green than Kenny G.

Atheism

Is it a religion? Some adherents act as if it is, defending their own un-belief in God or spiritual doctrine with the fervor of an evangelical. If you're one of the doubters looking to join the A-crowd, it's important first to distinguish yourself as a true atheist, rather than a more namby-pamby agnostic. Agnostics are the hedgers, the raised-as-one-thing-but-looking-for-something-grooviers, the ones who think there must be something out there but don't know if it looks like Allah or Yahweh or a reincarnated daffodil. If you're a true atheist, your "religion" is the world of science and observable phenomena. You take your creation story from Darwin, and your holy book is *On the Origin of Species*.

Lights Out

What happens after death is really just physics. More specifically, it's the first law of thermodynamics: In short, energy can neither be created nor destroyed, but only changed from one form to another. So when you kick the bucket, where does all your vivaciousness and energy go? Perhaps repurposed into putrid gases during decomposition? Converted into food for the fish? (Be warned: The gritty details of your available options might test your cynical mettle and send you searching for some other options.)

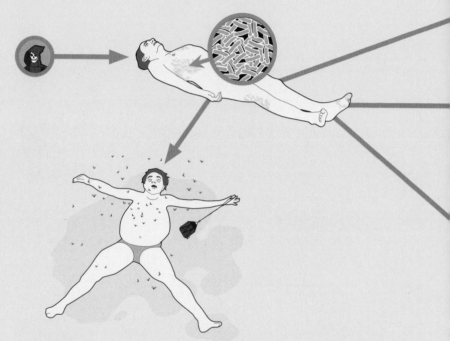

The Worms Crawl In

The old ditty that says "the worms play pinochle on your snout" is really a rather kind description of the basics of decomposition. Once you are dead, the live bacteria and digestive enzymes in your gut start agitating at their enclosure, finally breaking free to start digesting their only "food" option: your internal organs. And flies—this cannot be put delicately—start laying eggs in all your orifices; later they hatch into maggots. The fluids in your cavity then produce gases including (no joke) cadaverine and putrescine as by-products that bloat your body like a pool floatie. At this point, you reek, but to the insects, it's merely perfume, and the young maggots start tearing you apart with their mouth hooks, joined by beetles, mites, and wasps. Finally, your blackened body collapses and the fluids drain. It takes a while longer from this point for hair and skin to decompose. Sure you want to be an atheist?

Human Popsicle

For those of you with more faith in science than in God, **cryonics** preserves you at a cool -196° C (-321° F)—the boiling point of liquid nitrogen—after legal death has been pronounced (your heart has stopped beating). You are then stored in one of two American facilities. One glitch: The cooling causes irreversible damage to the body (no one has figured out the thawing yet). But hey, maybe molecular biology will catch up. If not, it's not like you believed life after death was possible anyway.

Envirodeath

Too green for burial or cremation? Try **Resomation**! In Resomation, the body is first placed in a silk bag, then encased in a metal cage, and finally loaded into a Resomator. This machine is filled with water and potassium hydroxide, and the contents are heated to a very high temperature in pressurized conditions, effectively dissolving your body and leaving behind liquid and calcium phosphate deposits called "bone shadows," then crushed into "bio-ash." Now you're ready to go back to your family, or to be used to water the roses.

YOU ARE HERE

Fish Food

Interestingly enough, people destined for cremation are still placed in a casket prior to being incinerated (seems like kind of a racket, but the cremation guy probably doesn't want to handle your lifeless body). Placed on the top level of the cremation chamber, your body burns at a temperature of over 1,600° F, hot enough to burn all but calcium deposits and bones, which drop to the lower level of the chamber. The whole process lasts for less time than a Duraflame takes to burn: about one-and-a-half hours if you're of average size. Once you cool, you're scanned for metal bits, from either your body or the coffin, and the remaining bones and calcium deposits are then milled into a sort of crematory flour—hence the conventional wisdom that the substance in the urn is ash.

Baha'i Faith

Espousing a progressive viewpoint (perhaps more acceptable today than it was at the time of its founding nearly 200 years ago), Baha'i focuses on the warm and fuzzy notion of the commonality and essential unity of all world religions. The six million followers believe God's divine revelations have already been channeled through all the big guys: Jesus, Muhammad, Buddha, Krishna, and Baha Ullah. If the last name doesn't ring a bell, it is because he is the most recent Messenger of God and, you guessed it, the official founder of the Baha'i faith. Baha Ullah appears to have been the original hippie, teaching his followers the supreme importance of religious tolerance and the value of respect, love, and friendship. At the heart of Baha'i is the fundamental notion that there is one religion, one truth, and that the soul's edification is the reason for all the fuss. As in the old parable about the blind men and the elephant, all of the world's religions have been describing parts of the ultimate truth without seeing the whole.

Come On, Baby, Light My Fire

As a group, the Baha'i engage in social-justice missions and are big advocates of developmental work in education, agriculture, and health care. These do-gooders are also committed to eliminating racism and sexism (*of course*), and are, not surprisingly, big fans of the United Nations. There is no clergy—instead members engage in homey "firesides," congregating at centers or in private homes to discuss the finer points of the religion, and practice individual prayer and meditation.

The Catch

There are no dietary restrictions, no mandatory tithing, nor many social restrictions; however, be warned: Alcohol is prohibited and monogamous marriage is a cornerstone of the faith. Swingers with a martini habit need not apply.

Moving On Up

Death is not final, but a continuation with a new existence in the spiritual realm—the soul continues to grow and learn after it has been freed from the confines of the body. So death is actually a plus. While not every soul is guaranteed the same level of success in the afterlife, there is no going backward in the beyond, only forward. A good afterlife puts you closer to God via spiritual enlightenment, and a bad one, predictably, distances you from Him. Thus, heaven and hell are simply relative conditions of the soul.

Buddhism

Maybe the reason this major world religion, with more than 300 million followers, has been around for 2,500 years is because it is refreshingly free of a supreme deity. It also doesn't hurt that in Buddhist thought death is not something to be feared, but is merely a way station in the cycle of birth and rebirth, or reincarnation. The physical body, in fact, is just another attachment to be shed in the quest for enlightenment or *nirvana*, the "state of liberation" for which all Buddhists strive. But there's a catch: What form you take in your next life depends on your actions during this lifetime. Positive deeds and thoughts build good merit, which in turn results in good karma, while negative actions result in the opposite.

If you haven't quite achieved enlightenment, there are six possible realms of existence for your next go-around.

Hungry Ghost

An excess of evil deeds lands you in this spiritual realm marked by endless desire with no possibility for satisfaction, like being stuck on a cross-country flight—forever. As in all the six realms of existence, if you endure your misery graciously, you can hope for an upgrade to a higher realm next time around.

Asura

This realm is reserved for a powerful lineup of demigods who are in constant battle with the gods of the lower heavenly realms. Obsessed with warfare, the asuras also possess many traits that go along with violent personalities, such as lust, pride, jealousy, and rage. While asuras have more power and enjoy more pleasurable circumstances than do humans, they are also less happy, consumed as they are with envy of the devas. Think Paris Hilton.

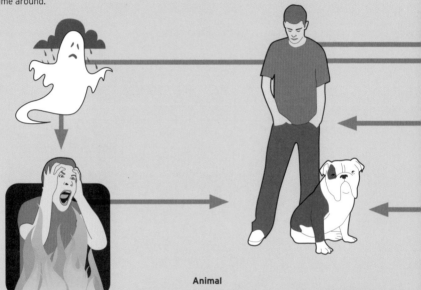

Animal

Eat a lot of hamburgers, and do a lot of other bad stuff, and you might end up as Rover. It's difficult for animals to attain enlightenment because of being forced to concentrate on their primal needs (and because of their itty-bitty brains). Nevertheless, be a good doggie and you may get to experience *samsara* (suffering) in human form. Think about that the next time you opt to sit on the couch instead of taking your dog out for a walk. You may be switching places in the next life.

Naraka/Hell

A realm not visible to humans, for good reason. You get what you give, and if you were, say, Pol Pot, you could end up in a constant state of pain and torture—for eons. Your only ticket out is doing your time and burning up that bad karma.

Nirvana

You made it! You are finally free of that darned cycle of birth and rebirth. You want for nothing, and therefore everything is yours. And, for a special bonus, enlightened beings (or Buddhas) get to experience a little heaven on earth. Nirvana is not only the end of rebirth after you die but the end of samsara while you are alive. Nirvana is basically a mind at perfect clarity and lucidity, free of attachment and its requisite suffering. So, game over. You're free!

Deva

Folks (really gods now) in this realm are free from material want and so can spend their time pursuing higher callings such as meditation, philosophy, art, and music. Imagine inhabiting the world of George Clooney and his pals at Lake Como. You get the picture, but don't get used to it. Unlike in nirvana, your stay is not eternal. You're here for sixteen million years, and not a day more.

Human

Enlightenment is most possible in this realm, as the conditions (including much suffering) are ripe for it. Of course, there is also the aforementioned suffering to bear. Really, it's *Groundhog Day,* with a twist. Karmic accumulation determines your new life, whether you're movin' on up or paying off some bad deeds from your previous life.

The Church of Christ, Scientist

A religion only Rambo could love, the Church of Christ, Scientist (more commonly and elegantly referred to as Christian Science) is definitely not for wimps—before or after death. Those averse to pain and suffering, and not just the existential kind, need not apply. Both your physical and spiritual health are up for debate: Founder Mary Baker Eddy claimed that the entire material world, including your corporeal body, is an illusion and, by extension, so are sickness and pain. Eddy's epiphany came after she was seriously injured from a fall in 1866. Reading the Book of Matthew in her sickbed, she came upon verse 9:2, "And, behold, they brought to him a man sick of the palsy, lying on a bed: and Jesus seeing their faith said unto the sick of the palsy; Son, be of good cheer; thy sins be forgiven thee." She was then immediately cured, and it was that experience that spurred her to launch the Church of Christ, Scientist, which got off the ground with the publication of the impenetrable *Science and Health with Key to the Scriptures*.

Ouch! Ouch!

Christian Scientists are hardcore: no Prozac, no painkillers, no docs, period. Broken leg? Pray on it. This isn't just the six-hours-into-the-stomach-flu-praying-to-the-Almighty-for-some-relief; this is the no-medicine, no-surgery, no-doctors, no-nothin' school of cold-turkey healing. You just need to adjust your expectations and behavior, and by purging ignorance, fear, and sin, you can cure all that ails you. Spiritual ruminations aside, statistics tell us that Christian Scientists seem to rejoin the spiritual realm slightly sooner than everyone else; death rates skew younger across the board for these folks.

Where's the Good Part?

If life is an illusion, so is death. Instead, your immortal spirit floats around town, like Jimmy Stewart in *It's a Wonderful Life*. But, wait, you say, I saw my Aunt Gladys at her funeral and she was, like, *cold* and her heart wasn't beating . . . was that an illusion? Christian Scientists do admit that humans *appear* to die, the "symptoms" of which signal the beginning of a rigorous spiritual self-improvement course that continues until all evil destroys itself.

Heaven or Hell

In keeping with Christian Scientists' aversion to binaries, they eschew heaven, believing it to be a state of consciousness, and think "hell" is self-created misery (like reading Sartre). Make sense? Didn't think so.

The Church of Jesus Christ of Latter-Day Saints

Mormon missionaries have a reputation for being as dogged as telemarketers in their efforts to show you the light. But when you die, you could find this a blessing rather than a curse. In fact, the Mormons might give you more chances to make it to heaven than any other religion. You've probably had plenty of chances to adopt LDS principles and accept Jesus. Really, probably *plenty*. But if you've been slow to join the fold, worry not. After you die, you'll still have access to education and coaching geared to guide your soul toward salvation.

In addition to wearing magic underpants (Mormons prefer to call these white skivvies "temple garments" or "God's Armor" and wear them to remind themselves of Mormon modesty), devout Mormons shun hot beverages and alcohol, and tithe a solid 10 percent of their earnings to the Church. Fans of *Big Love* should be reminded that polygamy is endorsed by neither the Church nor federal law—it's just TV, folks.

This Earthly Tabernacle Is Too Small

The Mormons believe a finite number of souls are red-shirted up in heaven, waiting for an infant to be born so they can inhabit its body. The new baby, or "earthly tabernacle," is just a tad too small to fit the "spiritual child" who flies down from heaven to occupy it. Just as with women trying to wear jeans two sizes too small, something's got to give. The spiritual children shed some extra weight by losing all memory of what it was like to live with Heavenly Father up there in the First Estate. That's why you can't quite recall the good life, nor any of the infinite past lives you have had.

Three Flavors of Heaven

With names that sound like fun-seeking triplets on spring break, the **Celestial**, **Terrestrial**, and **Telestial Kingdoms** make up the three degrees of Mormon heaven. The most posh by far is the **Celestial**. You get a cache of wives, your own planet, and a chance to father more spiritual children.

You Were Warned

Don't do it. *Don't!* There is only one unpardonable LDS sin, that of blaspheming the Holy Spirit. To do so means even after the Resurrection you must suffer the wrath of God forever. It's only the truly horrid who will remain to hang with the Sons of Perdition, the ominous moniker you gain as an inhabitant of hell, who so far count only Lucifer and Cain. By all accounts, these two are pretty poor company, as mopey and boring as the guy who's just broken up with the best girlfriend he ever had. You really are a loser.

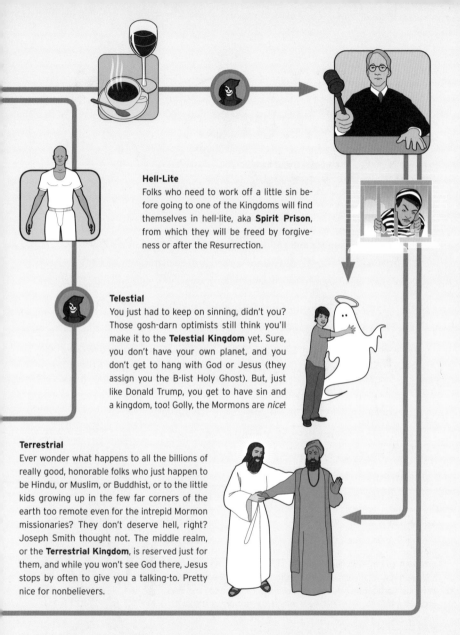

Hell-Lite

Folks who need to work off a little sin before going to one of the Kingdoms will find themselves in hell-lite, aka **Spirit Prison**, from which they will be freed by forgiveness or after the Resurrection.

Telestial

You just had to keep on sinning, didn't you? Those gosh-darn optimists still think you'll make it to the **Telestial Kingdom** yet. Sure, you don't have your own planet, and you don't get to hang with God or Jesus (they assign you the B-list Holy Ghost). But, just like Donald Trump, you get to have sin and a kingdom, too! Golly, the Mormons are *nice*!

Terrestrial

Ever wonder what happens to all the billions of really good, honorable folks who just happen to be Hindu, or Muslim, or Buddhist, or to the little kids growing up in the few far corners of the earth too remote even for the intrepid Mormon missionaries? They don't deserve hell, right? Joseph Smith thought not. The middle realm, or the **Terrestrial Kingdom**, is reserved just for them, and while you won't see God there, Jesus stops by often to give you a talking-to. Pretty nice for nonbelievers.

The Church of Satan

You'd think belief in the devil (and, by extension, hell) would be a no-brainer for any self-respecting Satanist. Interestingly, the members of this most "branded" branch of Satanism, the Church of Satan, founded by the notorious Anton LaVey, actually behave more like Christopher Hitchens with pointy eyebrows than any devil-worshipping, goat-sacrificing servant of the Dark Lord. LaVey started the Church of Satan in San Francisco *(where else?)* in 1966 *(of course!)*, having evolved from a group called the Order of the Trapezoid. Lots of artists, writers, and other ne'er-do-wells joined, and the media ate it all up. LaVey charismatically ran his church until his death in 1997. His wife and an appointed Magus now carry on his dream. Ironically, these folks do not actually believe in Satan as an entity, but more as a metaphor for man's true, carnal nature. If your heart's set on an afterlife, however, you should probably look elsewhere—Satanism is all about enjoying the here and now and not holding on to pathetic, "self-delusional pipe dreams" of some great hereafter.

Calling All Hedonists

In outlining what the metaphoric Satan stands for, the *Satanic Bible* lays down the official Nine Satanic Statements. Highlights include "Satan represents indulgence instead of abstinence," and "Satan represents kindness to those who deserve it instead of love wasted on ingrates." There are, surprisingly, also Nine Satanic Sins, including stupidity, pretentiousness, lack of perspective, and even lack of aesthetics. The mostly commonsensical Eleven Satanic Rules include not giving unwanted advice or treating your friends like unpaid therapists, as well as several involving proper "lair" etiquette. The Rules also advise you to curtail sexual advances unless you get the "mating signal." Emily Post would be proud.

The Pros and Cons of Devil Worship

Satanists are not only sybaritic but are in the unapologetically smash-the-other-cheek camp (which is a pro or con, depending on your nature). Plus you get to have sex as much as you want and still not go to hell. Actually, you won't go anywhere. Death is simply the end. In the words of LaVey, "Life is the great indulgence—death the great abstinence. Therefore, make the most of life here and now!"

YOU ARE HERE

Confucianism

For you don't-worry-be-happy folks, Confucianism offers intellectual stimulation and satisfying rituals without the burdens of prayer, gods, and guilt. Based on the teachings of early Chinese philosopher Confucius, it plays nice with Buddhism and Taoism, both of which provide a greater spiritual dimension (should you yearn for that) to the teachings of the great man. Left-brainers will dig the OCD focus on numbers, and those who like to entrust their decision-making to anyone but themselves will find using the *I Ching* (an ancient Chinese text used like a Magic 8 Ball™) to be enormously satisfying.

In general, Confucius's teachings focus on the importance of ritual, family, honesty, righteousness, benevolence, and loyalty to country. And since it is more an ethical system than a religion, Confucianism is most concerned with rituals and one's correct conduct through the four distinct life phases: birth, maturity, marriage, and death.

Birth

The spirit of the fetus, T'ai-shen, deals harshly with anyone who harasses the mother-to-be. Baby's got your back.

Reaching Maturity

Frankly, kind of a letdown. No bar mitzvahs here; the most you can hope for is a chicken dinner.

Marriage

A much bigger deal, apparently, than maturation, as there are no fewer than six distinct stages (proposal, engagement, dowry, procession, marriage and reception, and the morning after), each accompanied by an elaborate ritual. No need for a wedding planner—Confucius has it covered. Particularly curious about that morning-after ritual? Despite what you might be thinking, it involves the bride serving breakfast to the groom's parents, after which they reciprocate the favor.

Love Those Rituals

While decidedly vague on the afterlife, Confucianism is quite specific about the rituals surrounding death. After the dearly departed has departed, loved ones holler out to the neighbors, like the nonnas in the Bronx, to inform the community of the event. Then the family puts on their grubbies and washes the body before placing it in the coffin. Perks include the expectation that mourners will bring gifts and money to help offset funeral costs. A willow branch, meant to represent the soul of the deceased, accompanies the body through the burial ritual.

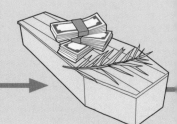

Dodgy on the Hereafter

"But am I going to hell?" you ask. Who knows, pilgrim. Confucius, although a terribly cute old man, was rather vague on the nature of the afterlife. Confucius apparently refused to entertain any discussions regarding magic, devils, hell, or heaven. When an impulsive disciple had the pluck to ask more specifically about the hereafter, the Master answered, "Till you know about the living, how are you to know about the dead?" 'Nuf said.

Confucius did put a lot of import on ancestor worship, though, perhaps more out of his great love of family than from any belief in the power of those beyond to affect the lives of those on earth. Either way, it's always best to cover your bases. Confucianists give their deceased family members a great deal of attention. During the Festival of Hungry Ghosts, celebrated on the fifteenth night of the seventh lunar moon, families even take care of other families' ancestors. On the day of the festival, people set out food and wine in front of their homes in order to satisfy any former inhabitants who have been neglected by their own peeps and therefore might be tempted to cause some trouble.

Druze Faith

The Druze are a mysterious and incredibly exclusive group, harder to work than the rope line at a hot L.A. club. Originally centered in Lebanon, Israel, and Syria, the Druze enjoy a worldwide following today as an offshoot of Islam with some Gnostic, Neo-Platonic, and even a little Sufi thought thrown into the mix. And with its promise of reincarnation instead of the crapshoot of paradise or seven levels of hell, you might be itching to sign up. Unfortunately, the Druze closed the membership doors in the year 1042 and, unless you have a hereditary birthright, you cannot convert or marry into this religion.

Even if you are lucky enough to be a bona fide Druze, chances are you won't hang out in the VIP section anyway. About 80 percent of the Druze are part of the Ignorant, and are not allowed access to the six holy texts (intriguingly rumored to reveal secrets from the Quran, the Bible, and the Torah).

Pork, polygamy, and profanity are general no-no's for the Druze while it is required that all Druze recognize Al-Hakim bi-Amr Allah (an eleventh-century Fatimid caliph considered the manifestation of God) and adhere to monotheism.

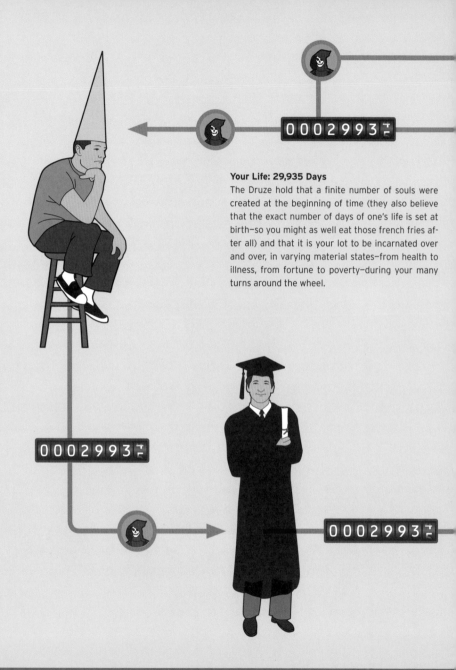

Your Life: 29,935 Days

The Druze hold that a finite number of souls were created at the beginning of time (they also believe that the exact number of days of one's life is set at birth—so you might as well eat those french fries after all) and that it is your lot to be incarnated over and over, in varying material states—from health to illness, from fortune to poverty—during your many turns around the wheel.

Heaven

Heaven is a spiritual realm and represents a time when the individual soul has reached purification and unites with the Cosmic (or Universal) Mind, *al-aaqal al kulli*.

Hell

Instead of being a place, hell is a spiritual condition wherein you feel far from God and, though you long to be closer, you can't quite get there. Kind of like trying to lose those last ten pounds.

Eckankar

The benefits for followers of this New Age religion—founded in 1965 by Paul Twitchell—include reams of written materials and study guides to steer you toward your spiritual liberation, religious colleagues more gung-ho than PTA moms at a bake sale, and a funky little practice called "Soul Travel," which allows you to explore the hidden Inner Planes. The cons: Well, besides the unfortunate moniker "ECKist," Soul Travel, as promising as it sounds, is a lot like a Native American peyote trip, without the peyote. Through Soul Travel you learn, by practicing spiritual excercises, to block out the crazy physical world and fly to your inner core. The goal of all ECKists is to achieve liberation from the cycle of reincarnation in this lifetime, enabling one to become God's "conscious coworker." You could do worse for an office buddy, though one would suspect He will consistently show you up at review time.

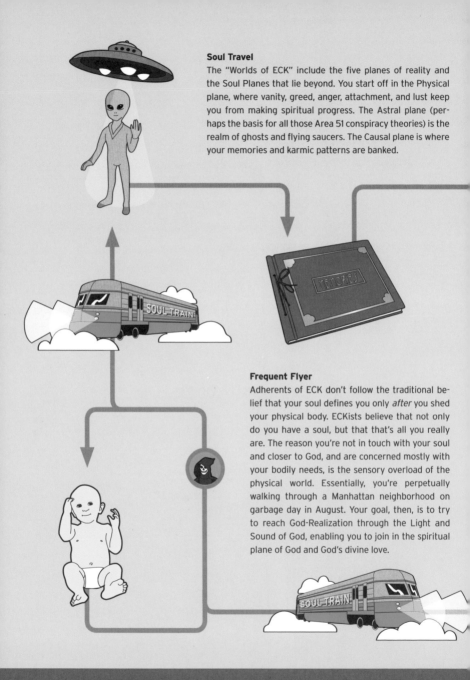

Soul Travel

The "Worlds of ECK" include the five planes of reality and the Soul Planes that lie beyond. You start off in the Physical plane, where vanity, greed, anger, attachment, and lust keep you from making spiritual progress. The Astral plane (perhaps the basis for all those Area 51 conspiracy theories) is the realm of ghosts and flying saucers. The Causal plane is where your memories and karmic patterns are banked.

Frequent Flyer

Adherents of ECK don't follow the traditional belief that your soul defines you only *after* you shed your physical body. ECKists believe that not only do you have a soul, but that that's all you really are. The reason you're not in touch with your soul and closer to God, and are concerned mostly with your bodily needs, is the sensory overload of the physical world. Essentially, you're perpetually walking through a Manhattan neighborhood on garbage day in August. Your goal, then, is to try to reach God-Realization through the Light and Sound of God, enabling you to join in the spiritual plane of God and God's divine love.

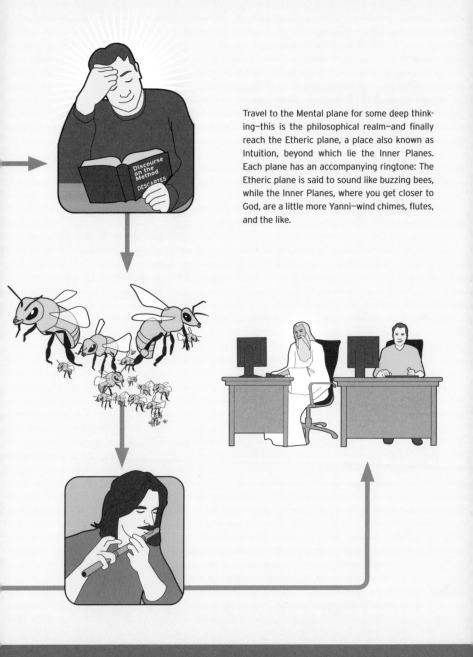

Travel to the Mental plane for some deep thinking—this is the philosophical realm—and finally reach the Etheric plane, a place also known as Intuition, beyond which lie the Inner Planes. Each plane has an accompanying ringtone: The Etheric plane is said to sound like buzzing bees, while the Inner Planes, where you get closer to God, are a little more Yanni—wind chimes, flutes, and the like.

Gnosticism

If Methodists are Baptists who can read, as the old joke goes, then Gnostics are Christianity's Advanced Placement students. Deriving their name from the Greek word *gnōsis*, meaning "knowledge," the Gnostics place greater importance in book smarts than on faith, dismiss sin as *so Old Testament*, and have a very different outlook on the nature of God as revealed in the Bible from that of their Jesus-loving brethren. You can see why traditional Christians wouldn't cotton to these notions and why, while Gnostics have been around as long as St. Peter, the early Christian Church tried hard to keep them on the down-low. The Church's official position on Gnostics (*Gnostic who?*), along with the sect's inherently academic nature, have always made it a hard sell.

The Gnostics assert that Jehovah of Hebrew scripture (the leading man in the Bible) was born of Sophia, the angel of wisdom. Junior (or Demiurge, as they call him) then created earth, the universe, and human beings. Despite Demiurge's accomplishments, he remains unaware of the existence of the High God and doesn't even know who his own mom is! This shocking ignorance is the reason life on earth is less than paradisaical.

Gimme Gnosis

For Gnostics, the physical body, and indeed the universe, is a prison, a kind of hell that you can only escape through death. A loophole exists, however, in the transformative nature of knowledge that allows humans to see the folly of attachments and glimpse the true and brilliant nature of things.

So Jesus and Buddha Walk into a Bar . . .

At the end of your life, the Gnostics say, death will release the soul from its physical prison and, if proper enlightenment was achieved in mortal life, your soul will travel across the universe to merge with the High or True God. If you were remiss in your studies (or believed that line the other Christians threw at you), back into another bodily prison you go to try it all again.

Sin

The only real sin is ignorance; ergo, salvation comes in the form of knowledge. It is not through Jesus's suffering and death that you will be saved, but by sharing in his teachings and the wisdom he imparted.

$$slope[x\_] := x/Sqrt[64 - x^2]$$

$$f(s) - f(x)$$

$$\lim_{s \to} $$

Sound Familiar?

Wait, you're saying they believe in a cycle of rebirth into an imperfect world of suffering, broken only by the acquisition of true wisdom, or enlightenment? Hmmm, sound familiar? Like a certain Eastern religion fond of saffron robes, *japa malas*, and meditation? Perhaps the Church didn't do a perfect job of keeping this one quiet.

Greek Orthodox

Aside from those simple black robes and hats that resemble a chef's toque—oh, and that whole Julian calendar thing—are there really any differences between the Greek Orthodox and the Roman Catholic Church? Hell, yes! No purgatory, for one. The Assyrian and Oriental Orthodox cried "foul" on that first, way back in 451 CE. Boy, was that a mess. One side said Jesus was both human and divine, and the other said he was just divine. Seem like a minor point? Well, has it ever made you mad when someone put the toilet paper roll on the wrong way? In 1054 they got into it again, this time over the nature of the Trinity. The result was more of a divorce than a separation. And thus the Eastern Orthodox Church—of which the Greek Orthodox is a part—was born.

So if you're Greek, you've got a 90 percent chance of already being a Greek Orthodox, and if you're not Greek, roasted lamb and *spanakopita* might tempt you into converting. Although it's true the Greek Orthodox love their feasts, you should know they also love their fasts—the most extreme abstain from red meat, dairy products, wine, and olive oil for nearly 180 days a year, though they do get a break on the weekend before Easter.

You Might Want to Start Praying

When you die, your soul may hang out for a while on earth awaiting the Temporary Judgment. You'll get a little taste of what either hell or heaven would be like, your choices following the Final Judgment, and the resurrection of your body.

Here's where being nice to your family comes in: The righteous can intercede right up until the Final Judgment, swaying the outcome like a phone call from the governor can commute a death sentence.

To Know Him Is to Love Him

The Orthodox do believe, like other Christians, that resurrected souls will be reunited with their resurrected bodies. But they also think there will be positive progression after Final Judgment toward a deeper love of God—not just fire-torment-screaming or floating-angels, bingo!

Hell is more ignorance of God's incredible and infinite love than a hot pit of despair. With a hell like that, who needs purgatory?

They Love Them Their Saints

For those craving the ritual and fetishistic aspect of Catholicism, the Greek Orthodox Church won't disappoint. Everyone in heaven is a saint, according to the Orthodox, though they still think there are a few standouts that deserve special veneration (through bas-reliefs, candles, and other gift-store kitsch). When a saint is revealed and officially recognized (glorification), he or she gets his or her own day, special hymns, and his or her own icons.

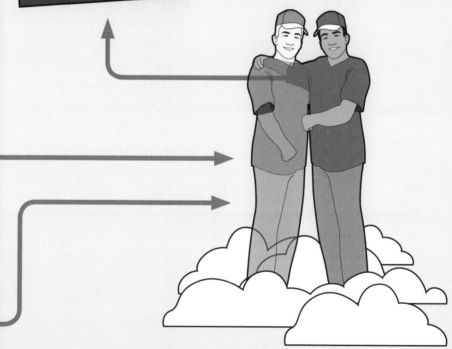

Hinduism

You don't get to be the world's oldest practiced religion by being unrealistic. Hinduism recognizes the inherent temptations of *samsara* (that revolving door of birth, life, death, and rebirth) and, like a good parent, outlines clear rules for its many children in how to obtain *moksha* (freedom from samsara). Though there are many Hindu sects, featuring a colorful cast of deities—the multi-armed Lord Shiva, the elephant-headed god Ganesh, the ferocious goddess Kali—and a complex and wide-ranging belief system, there are a few ideas that are universally accepted. These include the endlessly-fun-to-repeat trio of dharma, karma, and samsara, as well as the practice of yoga (as a path to moksha).

While Hindus can't even agree if they are monotheistic or polytheistic, they all pretty much believe in the existence within each individual of a soul or spirit called the *atman* (or *jiva*). The atman is indistinguishable from the Brahman, or the supreme spirit, the infinite and transcendent reality that is the basis for the known and unknown world. Once you get this idea, you've passed. That's it—the whole meaning of life. You have reached moksha. Well, maybe it is not quite so easy.

To know is one thing; to do, another. Samsara has its pleasures (eating ice cream, having tantric sex), and while ephemeral, they're fun, distracting people from the path toward moksha.

Lots of Dharma = Good Karma

Karma is, of course, a major factor in the afterlife equation. Good deeds earn you reincarnation into a higher station. Because Hindus follow the controversial caste system—consisting of Brahmins, Ksatriyas, Vaishyas, Shudras, and Untouchables—there is no pulling yourself up by the bootstraps and transcending your social status in this lifetime. Being naughty, on the other hand, translates into a downgrade on your next spin. Your exact thoughts at the moment of death also factor into the equation. (Hint: While crossing against oncoming traffic, keep your mind on God.) Karma also affects your choice of "waiting room" in the form of one of many heavens and hells described in Hindu scriptures. What options! These varying levels of heaven and hell are not final destinations, as in Christianity, but simply layovers on your way to another go-around in samsara (while a liberated soul—one who has reached moksha—gets a nonstop flight to Brahman).

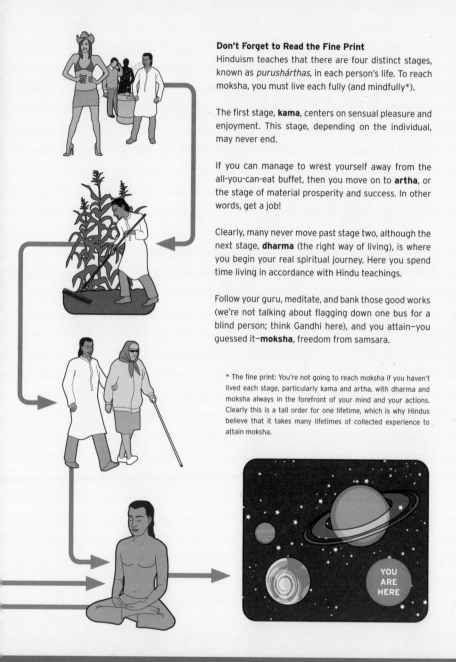

Don't Forget to Read the Fine Print

Hinduism teaches that there are four distinct stages, known as *purushárthas*, in each person's life. To reach moksha, you must live each fully (and mindfully*).

The first stage, **kama**, centers on sensual pleasure and enjoyment. This stage, depending on the individual, may never end.

If you can manage to wrest yourself away from the all-you-can-eat buffet, then you move on to **artha**, or the stage of material prosperity and success. In other words, get a job!

Clearly, many never move past stage two, although the next stage, **dharma** (the right way of living), is where you begin your real spiritual journey. Here you spend time living in accordance with Hindu teachings.

Follow your guru, meditate, and bank those good works (we're not talking about flagging down one bus for a blind person; think Gandhi here), and you attain—you guessed it—**moksha**, freedom from samsara.

* The fine print: You're not going to reach moksha if you haven't lived each stage, particularly kama and artha, with dharma and moksha always in the forefront of your mind and your actions. Clearly this is a tall order for one lifetime, which is why Hindus believe that it takes many lifetimes of collected experience to attain moksha.

YOU
ARE
HERE

International Society for Krishna Consciousness

If you wear bright colors well, don't have a taste for steak, and gravitated toward the drum circle in college, the International Society for Krishna Consciousness, a hippie-era American offshoot of Hinduism (better known to many as "the crazy folks in saffron robes dancing in the airport"), could be your ticket. While the Andrew Weil-approved diet may improve your health, the daily recitation of the Krishna purification mantra—meant to be chanted for sixteen rounds each of a string of *mala,* or prayer beads (totaling 1,728 recitations per day)—might just kill you.

Happy Birthday, #48,003 . . .

As in many Eastern religions, Krishnas believe in transmigration: When you die you will be placed in the womb of your next mother, whose identity depends on your consciousness at the moment of death. So, having "Hare Krishna" on your lips at the time of your passing isn't a bad plan. Achieving Krishna consciousness earns your "imperishable soul" a spin with the Godhead, while more base thoughts earn you an appropriate rebirth. With 8,400,000 species of life in all, there should be a womb to suit you. Human consciousness (thinking about taxes and politics) earns you another human body, while animal consciousness (hankering for a sandwich) gets you an animal manifestation.

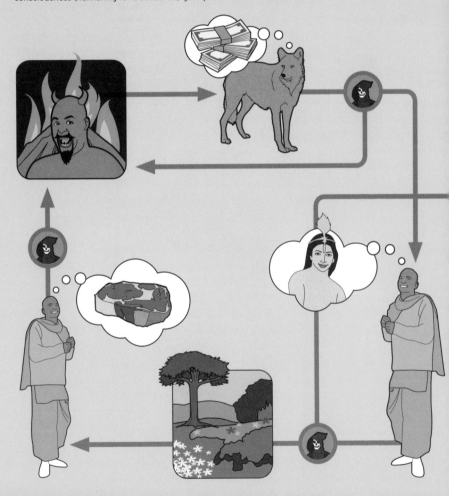

Heaven

According to the Krishna guru, there are many heavenly planets within our own material realm that are better than earth and populated by more beautiful people than you or your friends and family (like the French Riviera). If you were thinking pure thoughts at the time of your death, you might get to go to one. One can live there for millions of years, hobnobbing with the more-attractive and less-mortal while eating good food. But you can't stay there forever, and since you haven't achieved Godhead, you'll be joining the rest of us back on earth at some point in the future.

Hell

Carry sin on the brain, and you will go to hell. And the Krishnas don't play nice. They believe you commit sin by harvesting vegetables to make a meal (or by stepping inadvertently on ants), not to mention raping and pillaging and cutting in line. Does that standard seem unattainable? Live your life with an eye toward pleasing Krishna, and you'll be OK. Note: Unlike confessing, chanting the Krishna mantra doesn't "undo" *intentional* sin. (If you want a get-out-of-jail-free card, see Catholicism.)

Godhead

By achieving Krishna consciousness you get to see, hear, and play with Krishna, your friend and Supreme Godhead, your new BFF. Identifying Him should be easy—in pictures he's often portrayed as a bright blue boy, like a Hindu version of Grover.

Goin' Up to the Spirit in the Sky

According to Krishna guru Srila Prabhupada, the heaven that Jesus was talking about (yes, Krishnas are cool with Jesus) is a spiritual firmament far beyond the heavens of our own sky, wherein lie spiritual planets ruled over by various forms of Krishna. The supreme planet of this spiritual sky is called Goloka Vrndavana.

Islam

You think you've got Islam all figured out, don't you? Fundamentalist jihadists, praying to Mecca, cavorting virgins in paradise for the righteous—easy as pie, right? Not so fast. The world's second-largest religion is more complex than you might think. There's paradise, yes, and seven levels of Janna, or heaven, and a handful of deal-breakers, called the Five Pillars, that you must follow to get there. Islam involves almost as many rules as Judaism (with steeper afterlife penalties), including a monthlong "holiday" that makes being vegan sound indulgent, and some major hiking. And Allah is watching. At puberty, right when you're at your most vulnerable to peer pressure, he opens a sort of moral bank account for you, with all of your credits and debits scrupulously recorded for the mother of all audits come Judgment Day. The Muslims also throw in a pretty harsh booby prize—a stay in hell spent drinking pus, with a torment that sounds a lot like eternal death by Ebola. While there are many religions more suited for slackers and sinners, could 1.5 billion believers be wrong? Maybe. But do you really want to take your chances?

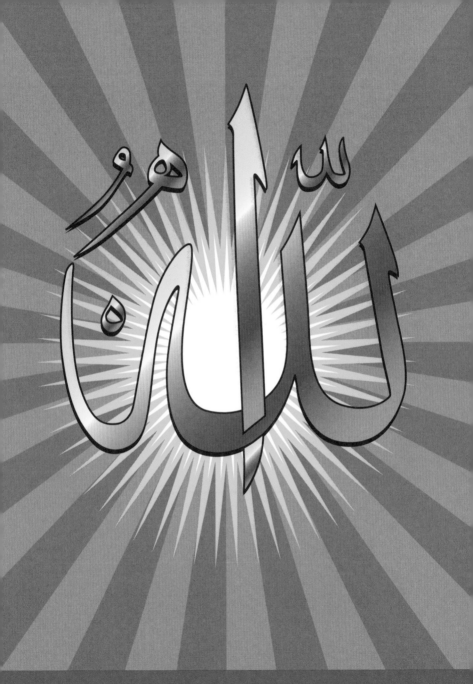

The Five Pillars

For every Muslim there are five duties necessary for making Allah happy and getting to heaven, like the chores your parents made you do in exchange for use of the family Buick. They include 1. **Hajj** (once during your lifetime, you need to make a pilgrimage to Mecca—easier done the closer you are to Mecca), 2. **Zakah** (Allah wants you to share with the less fortunate—c'mon, give it up), 3. **Sawm** (during the ninth month of the Islamic calendar, also known as Ramadan, from dawn till dusk you don't get to do anything fun, to remind you that Allah is totally righteous), 4. **Shahadah** (translation: Allah is righteous, like totally and completely righteous, and he and only he is totally and completely righteous), and 5. **Salah** (five times a day, you need to face Mecca and acknowledge that Allah is totally righteous).

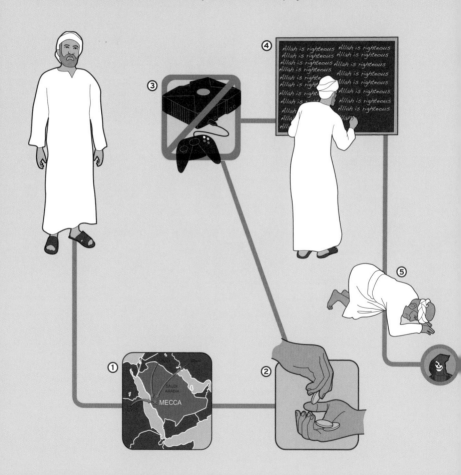

Make a Wish

Al-Firdaws is the center and highest (seventh) level of heaven, sometimes referred to as Paradise or Eden. The Prophet Muhammad is first in line to enter, then the poor, then the do-gooders. Other prophets can be found in other levels, where heaven is like attending a family reunion with only the relatives you like, plus lots of jewels, wine, and good-smelling things. The edge of the seventh heaven is marked by a lotus tree, Sidrat al-Muntaha—a far better sight than the tree whose roots dig into hell. (Shi'a Muslims believe that only Muhammad, his daughter, and the twelve Shi'a Imams have the ability to achieve Paradise.) Descriptions of heaven vary from having seven to 500 levels, some featuring pearl mansions and trees of gold; yet most agree that Allah's throne sits above Al-Firdaws. And yes, along with all the bling come the infamous virgins, aka "houris."

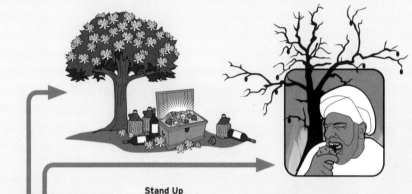

Stand Up

Your physical body is re-formed on the day of atonement, or the Day of Standing Up. Until then, your eternal soul hangs out awaiting resurrection and judgment in a sort of twilight slumber. While you're waiting, if you find yourself scratching like a dog with fleas, it doesn't bode well: Muslims believe you get a hint of your future destiny from the moment you die. Remember that moral bank account? It's time to cash in. Is it on to endless spiritual and physical pleasure? Or eternal torment? Take a stroll on the catwalk over hell to find out. If your conscience is too heavy, down, down you go.

Hell, or Jahannam, gets a lot of play in the Quran. Seven doors lead to a fiery pit, at the bottom of which grows the tree Zaqqum. The damned are made to eat the bitter fruit of the tree, which, according to different interpretations, either boils like water in their bellies or tears their bodies apart, causing their wounds to weep. As an added bonus, the damned are made to drink the aforementioned seeping pus. Yum. Now you know why the term "devout Muslim" is so ubiquitous. Doesn't it make you want to follow the Five Pillars?

Jainism

Tofu-munching greeners will appreciate the attention paid to all God's creatures, in life and beyond, by the Jains, a group of PETA-approved super-vegans who practice one of the oldest religions in the world and make up a powerful minority in India. Smartly avoiding all of that hubbub about Intelligent Design, the Jains simply take as a given that the universe and everything in it is eternal. Nothing that currently exists was ever created, or can ever be destroyed. If you can get rid of that pesky karma holding you back, following your death your perfectly uncreated and eternal soul can achieve liberation, or *moksha*. It should be said that while the Jains are perhaps most famous for wearing masks over their mouths to avoid accidentally inhaling small insects (who also have souls), the belief is that only humans can achieve moksha.

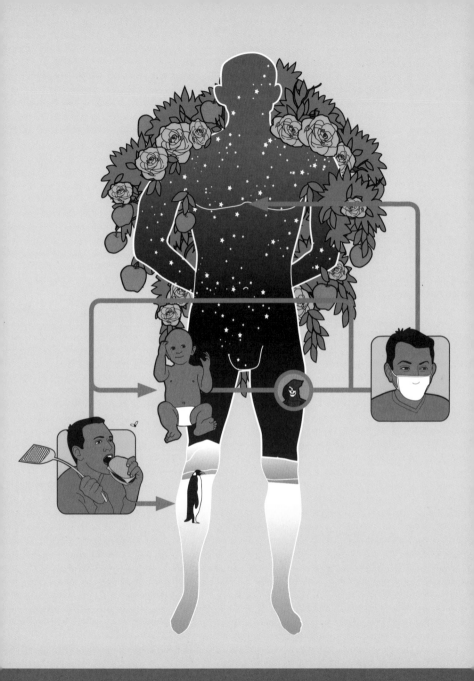

Just Sitting Under the Rose-Apple Tree

While the Christians believe man was made in God's image, the Jains turn that on its head, in a way, and envision a universe shaped like a standing man, legs spread, arms akimbo. Right around this gentleman's nipples you'll find the *deva loka*, or heavens, the highest level of which contains the enlightened souls who have achieved moksha and have been freed of the reincarnation cycle.

Moving down the body and alighting at his narrow waist is where all the rest of the soul-containing creatures, and the known world, are found. The exact location, if you must know, is called the Bharat Kshetra of the southern Jambudvipa. All this really means is that all the stuff with souls roams around his belly button. As an informational note, the literal translation of Jain Universe Man's middle is "Continent of the Rose-Apple Tree." Now *that's* someone who's secure in his manhood.

Hell Freezes Over

And, yes, everything your mother told you is true: The *narka loka*, or hells, are all found below the waist. Fitting for the Jains, who practice either chastity or strict monogamy, the narka loka are described as cold, dark, and icy. Since Jains are really about the moksha, though, you won't spend much time in hell. Freeze off a little karmic debt through spiritual cryotherapy and off you go to be reborn in a suitable form.

Soul Food

Jains believe *jiva*, or the soul, is found not only in humans but also in that fly you swatted this morning in your kitchen. However, jivas are separated into two main categories—immobile single-sensed, and mobile multi-sensed souls. They are divided again by the elements for the single-sensed and by the senses for the, well, sensate. For example, a Japanese maple tree contains a one-souled, plant-bodied, immobile, single-sensed jiva, while root vegetables, not eaten by the Jains, fall into the same classification save that they are multi-souled. The common louse, on the other hand, would qualify as a three-sensed, mobile jiva. If all of this has you reliving the taxonomic hell of your tenth-grade biology class, just keep it simple: Don't kill anything, hit anything, or even pinch. The idea of *ahimsa*, or nonviolence extended to all jivas, is perhaps the most fundamental principle of Jainism. The lesson here? Use your words, or risk heavy karmic buildup.

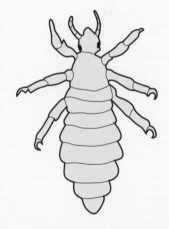

Jehovah's Witnesses

Some mainstream Christians get cranky when you lump Jehovah's Witnesses in with their faith, pointing out the rather large differences of opinion between this late nineteenth-century upstart and the Catholic and Protestant biggies. For example, the Witnesses don't buy into that whole Trinity thing, refuse blood transfusions on religious grounds, and think Jesus already came back to earth in 1914. Perhaps some of the greatest disparity comes when in consideration of the afterlife. Witnesses reject the notion that when you die your everlasting soul either goes up to heaven or down a few floors to hell, believing instead that you cease to exist, and patiently wait in nothingness for the Resurrection and a thousand years of judgment. *Unless*, that is, you are one of the 144,000 VIP—no line, no waiting, just a straight shot to heaven. The odds for making the cut aren't good, but if you think you've got what it takes to crack the top 144,000, a Witness would be more than happy to sign you up, caring, as they do, *deeply*, for your spiritual welfare.

And the Winners Are . . .

According to Witnesses, these 144,000 most faithful will rule as kings with God in heaven (and assist with the sentencing of those who don't make the cut), rendering Judgment Day as messy and cutthroat as a Junior beauty pageant. The Witnesses make you work for it, requiring righteousness, obedience to all of Jesus's commands (they take the Bible as the literal word of God), and a complete dedication to God and service in his army. This includes, you guessed it, witnessing, or spreading the Good (or not so good) Word to all of your friends, neighbors, and anyone else who will open his or her door to you.

Dust to Dust

No one ever said life was fair, and Witnesses go one step further, arguing that God never said anything about life after death, either. The Bible doesn't offer the promise of an immortal soul at all, but instead a long-term plan that enables spiritually resurrected humans to live eternally on a re-formed planet. Short term, death brings one of three options. Those who commit unpardonable sins (like leaving out carrots for Santa's reindeer), go straight to Gehenna, a place of total annihilation. Major ass-kissers could go straight on up to heaven, unless those 144,000 spots are already taken. Those middlin' billions who fall somewhere between heaven and Gehenna will wait in nothingness in Hades, humankind's common grave, for the Apocalypse and the ensuing 1,000 years of judgment.

Habitat for Humanity

According to Witnesses, the world following Armageddon comes off like a cross between a community garden project and an episode of *Survivor.* Those who don't get a seat in heaven immediately following death may still get their due, or may be allowed a palatable Plan B in eternal life post-Judgment on a post-Apocalyptic, paradisaical planet even Al Gore could love. For a thousand years after the destruction of the world, a merry band of millions will commence a major beautification project. During that time, God and his co-rulers will be sifting through the resurrected spirits for those who make the cut.

Not a Chance in Hell

In general, the Witnesses worship a pretty wrathful god. Their main publication, *The Watchtower*, has been noted to feature colorful depictions of Armageddon where birds and beasts rip apart human flesh. Plus, Judgment "Day" lasts for a millennium, and, you have to admit, only letting .0021818 percent of the world's population in to heaven doesn't really give most folks a fighting chance. On the other hand, the Witnesses throw the losers a bone by rejecting the idea of hell and eternal punishment. Even the unfaithful will be given a chance to live in paradise on Earth following the Resurrection, and while unpardonable sins earn you Gehenna, is eternal nothingness really that much to fear? In fact, ideologically flexible atheists with a penchant for sin should note that since this is what you think happens when you die anyway, enlisting with the Witnesses could earn you a paradise bonus with nothing to lose.

Judaism

For a religion that offers such *minute* detail on the do's and don'ts of everyday life (there are 613 *mitzvot,* or rules, to follow), Judaism plays it coy when it comes to the nitty-gritty of the sweet hereafter. Folks who love the precision of Emily Post, however, will appreciate the well-defined specifications for grieving, for dressing the body, how to do your own hair, whether or not to pull the plug—it's all covered. In addition, you do get the basic assurance of a general afterlife plan that rewards good works (with several option packages), and the promise of some kickin' perks once the Messiah really comes back to Earth. You see, Jesus (despite being a Jew himself) just didn't do it for most of his people—he was too much of a peacenik to be the true *moshiach,* (literally, "the anointed one.") The Jews are still waiting for someone to surpass their first physical and spiritual patriarchs—Abraham, Isaac, and Jacob—who led the tribe about 2,000 years before Christianity got going. They're a patient people.

For Your Own Good

By most counts, Judaism is the choice for those willing to do their heavy lifting in the here-and-now. But while the list of 613 mitzvot may seem like a lot, many just make good common sense and could, for example, help you to avoid contracting mad cow disease *(Never eat the flesh of a beast that died of itself)* or landing on *Jerry Springer (Do not indulge in familiarities with relatives—such as kissing, embracing, winking, or skipping—which may lead to incest).* The full list comes from the Torah, combined with other rules the rabbis make up and some that have just always been custom, like Aunt Fran bringing the green-bean casserole to family gatherings.

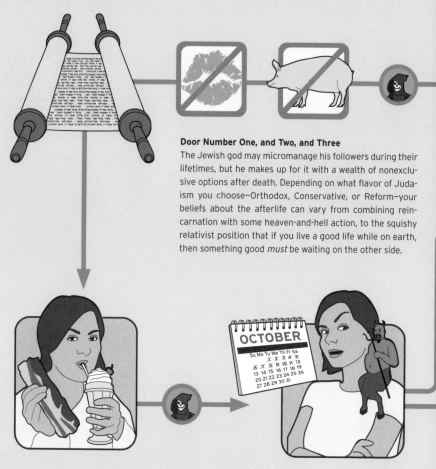

Door Number One, and Two, and Three

The Jewish god may micromanage his followers during their lifetimes, but he makes up for it with a wealth of nonexclusive options after death. Depending on what flavor of Judaism you choose—Orthodox, Conservative, or Reform—your beliefs about the afterlife can vary from combining reincarnation with some heaven-and-hell action, to the squishy relativist position that if you live a good life while on earth, then something good *must* be waiting on the other side.

Masochists Need Not Apply

Though the Jews share with Christians the irritable God of the Old Testament, pointy pitchforks and eternal hellfire have little place in Judaism's vision of eternity. Some Orthodox Jews believe there is a literal "Garden of Eden" (*Gan Eden*), a spiritual paradise said to offer sixty times the pleasure of a good *shabbos* (is that even *possible?*). Average Irving will probably go instead to Gehinnom, where for twelve fun-filled months less-than-perfect souls confront their personal demons (kind of like going home for the holidays).

Forget Jesus, Think . . . Obi-Wan Kenobi

The Jews dream of salvation by a Messiah who will embody every Jewish mom's dream for her son: He'll be a great political and military leader, charismatic and loved by all, and a righteous judge. Just ending wickedness, sin, and heresy is bound to fill his calendar, and gathering the exiles and restoring the line of King David might take a while, too. As one of God's foot soldiers, just sit back and wait for Resurrection, when you and the other good souls get to enjoy the perfect world you helped create. On the off chance you didn't buy into the Jewish notion of *tikkun olam,* or "mending the world," when you had the chance, the Resurrection instead signals your eternal off-ramp into nothingness.

Kabbalah

Behold the Kabbalah. You can score one of those red-string bracelets worn by the fashionistas—really a *bendel*, which protects against the evil eye. And, yes, you can also hang with Madonna (Esther to her fellow Kabbalah members), Winona Ryder, Courtney Love, and Ashton Kutcher, members of this second-century mystical branch of Judaism that's all the rage with the rich, famous, and infamous. But hold your horses. Before you start meditating on the seventy-two names of God (a popular Kabbalah ritual), you should be clear on what kind of afterlife you and the Material Girl have to look forward to. If you're looking for celeb access, be aware that you and Madonna will probably be on parallel paths—even in the afterlife. The Kabbalists subscribe to a kind of tracked reincarnation cycle, with enlightenment and a form of earthly nirvana being the final goal.

Tree of Life

For those who learn best with visual aids, Kabbalah has the handy Tree of Life diagram to help you interpret this rather complex belief system. The tree represents both the Kabbalist vision of creation and a step-by-step guide to personal enlightenment. The tree places the beginnings of the universe just above the Sephiroth of Ein Sof (basically, God's essence–meaning simultaneously nothingness and limitlessness). From this energy follows time and space, then wisdom (of a manly, yang sort), followed by the more reasoned (and feminine/yin) understanding, and so on until you take a round-trip back to beloved nothingness and reunite with the Divine (Ein Sof).

Gilgul

Early Kabbalists imagined all sorts of vivid heavenly realms, complete with angels, demons, dybbuks, and golems. Today, it is more common for followers to believe in the transmigration of the soul, or *gilgul*. The story goes that everyone possesses an ancient soul that has lived many lifetimes (and will live many more). Moving through the Tree of Life is no easy task, and one must be prepared to log many lifetimes before moving up a notch. Unlike your basic reincarnation, gilgul adheres to a kind of caste system for the afterlife. If you were a great and noble scholar in a past life, it follows you are also one now and will be reincarnated as such in future lives. Sucks for those destined to a long slog of it as telemarketers. For those folks, succor is offered in the form of pop-psychology-cum-spirituality in which a process of self-discovery softens the blow of a less-than-advantageous rebirth.

Lutheranism

While you might think of the Lutherans as a fairly benign bunch, they got their start, and their name, from a religious renegade. Because of a feisty little monk named Martin Luther, not only was an entire religious movement spawned, but your afterlife choices got fewer.

Back before dallying with altar boys was in the headlines, the Catholic Church was embroiled in a major scandal, allowing parishioners to reduce their time in purgatory by abusing a little loophole called "indulgences." The devout were originally given a partial remission of sin by doing tasks such as reciting prayers. But in 1517, Pope Leo X offered indulgences for parishioners who paid alms to view holy relics, such as milk from the Virgin Mary (who knew she pumped?) and straw from the baby Jesus's manger. For each alm, Catholics could have 100 days of purgatory knocked off—essentially allowing them to buy their way to heaven. Luther was outraged, and in a tizzy nailed his Ninety-five Theses to the Castle Church in Wittenberg, Germany. His theses not only exposed the abuse of indulgences but even questioned the divine power of the Pope.

Hail Mary Just Won't Cut It Anymore

While Catholics believe that nearly everyone stops in to purgatory after death, "paying off" lingering sin with punishment before going to heaven, Lutherans believe that if you have faith in Jesus Christ and accept him as your Lord (known as the "Doctrine of Justification"), when you die you will be whisked straight to the pearly gates. While this plays out well for the devout, the big-time sinners and all others who don't accept Jesus as their savior, well . . . you may wind up hankering for a belief system with a few more choices on the menu.

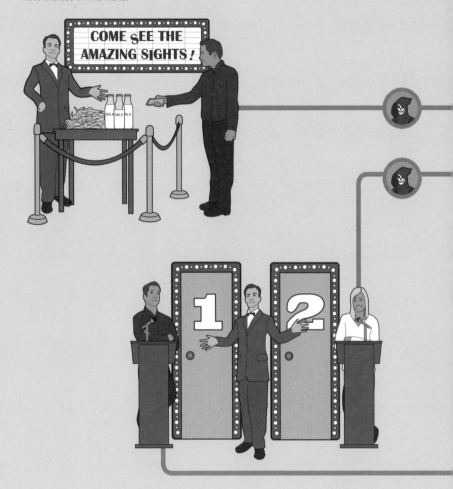

Are You Afraid? Really, Really Afraid?

Unlike some other Christians, Lutherans reject the notion that the soul sleeps until Judgment Day. While they agree that when Christ does rise again, your soul will be reunited with your resurrected body, the Lutheran faithful don't have to wait until then to enjoy the rewards of heaven. One of Martin Luther's theses, in fact, said that a person should be relieved of all penalties upon death (though mortal sinners and nonbelievers would still go straight to hell), because death in and of itself is enough to harsh your mellow. He also postulated that purgatory is unnecessary because fear of hell should be enough to keep you on the straight and narrow. (Luther wasn't right about everything.)

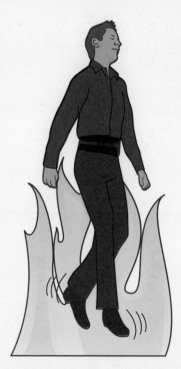

Door Number One or Door Number Two

This stripped-down religion offers only two afterlife plans: eternal bliss, or hell and torment. Heaven involves a restored and glorified body (without lipo!), no sin, no conflict, and unending joy in God's love, while hell involves the conscious experience of indescribable torment, much like watching *Riverdance*.

Modern Druidism

Tree huggers, ex-drama geeks, and those who subscribe to the Society for Creative Anachronism newsletter will find much to love in Druidism, both in this realm and in any other. Loosely drawing from the traditions of the ancient Celts, Modern Druids believe in reincarnation, but they also embrace the idea of equally real but hierarchical realms of existence as destinations on your ladder of spiritual development. These lyrical but practical people embrace an agrarian version of karmic law, referred to as the Law of the Harvest (basically, you reap what you sow), so while there is no hell in any of these realms, bad behavior will come back to bite you in some form. These fun-loving bards don't even require you to choose between a monotheistic or polytheistic belief system. The equinox and the solstice are like the Christians' Christmas to them, and a taste for mead doesn't hurt.

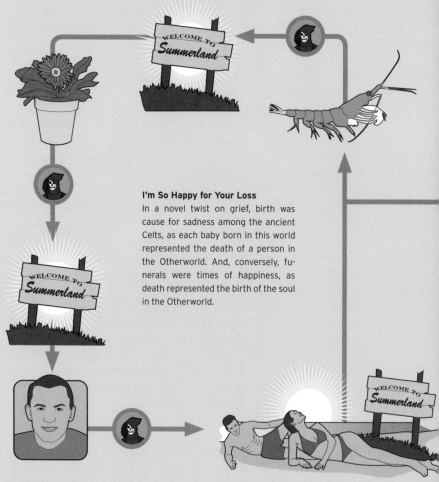

I'm So Happy for Your Loss

In a novel twist on grief, birth was cause for sadness among the ancient Celts, as each baby born in this world represented the death of a person in the Otherworld. And, conversely, funerals were times of happiness, as death represented the birth of the soul in the Otherworld.

The Apparent World

To the Druids, the world in which you are reading this book (sometimes called the Apparent World), is no more "real" than any of the other realms in the Otherworld. Your eternal soul could be reincarnated into another mortal shell—human, animal, or yes, lowly plant—to live yet another lifetime in the Apparent World, or you could be reincarnated into another realm in the Otherworld. After you have learned all that you can in this realm (probably harder if your soul is animating an entity with no central nervous system), you die and move on to a higher realm. As in a spiritual pyramid scheme, you keep moving up until you eventually rise to the highest realm, a place called the Source.

Summerland

Ancient Druids believed that the dead were transported to a place called the Otherworld by the unfortunately named god Bile (sometimes referred to as Bel or Belenus). Most Druids believe that after you die, you journey first to a destination called Summerland (or the Blessed Isles), a warm and sunny region in the Otherworld where you spend time visiting with friends and family in eternal summer until you are reincarnated.

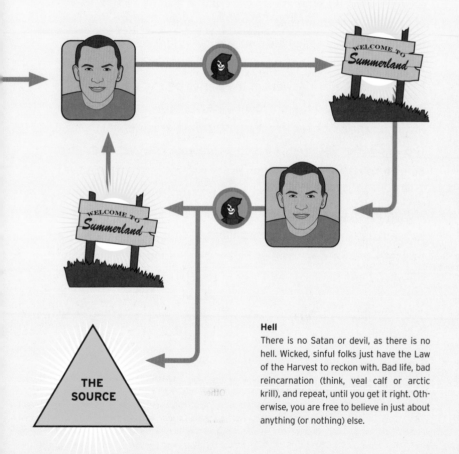

THE SOURCE

Hell

There is no Satan or devil, as there is no hell. Wicked, sinful folks just have the Law of the Harvest to reckon with. Bad life, bad reincarnation (think, veal calf or arctic krill), and repeat, until you get it right. Otherwise, you are free to believe in just about anything (or nothing) else.

Nation of Islam

Those expecting an afterlife experience worthy of the Nation of Islam rep—men in sharp black suits, guns blazing, the Man burning in a fiery hell of his own making—might be a little disappointed; this belief system plays less like *Pulp Fiction* than *Close Encounters*. While followers of the Nation of Islam, a movement more sociopolitical than religious, are primarily concerned with lifting up the black race on earth, they use traditional Islam as the inspiration for many of their teachings. However, they also believe Allah appeared in human form in founder Wallace Fard Muhammad in 1930, an idea that is abhorrent to traditional Muslims and constitutes a fundamental sin. In 1934, Fard (who subsequently disappeared—his identity and fate to remain a mystery to this day) named Elijah Muhammad (né Poole) the new head and Supreme Minister of the Nation of Islam.

Heaven on Earth

Nation of Islam rejects notions of resurrected bodies and verdant, paradisaical gardens, instead simply holding that life after death equals mental, but not physical, resurrection. While traditional Islam is very clear about the otherworldly heaven that awaits good Muslims, and the really nasty hell that awaits most everyone else, NOI's idea of heaven is a separate-but-equal America (contemporary race relations approximate their idea of hell). Nation of Islam and traditional Islam share humanitarian and strict moral practices as parts of their belief systems—from helping the poor and destitute to abstaining from drugs and alcohol. NOI followers also think the Quran, and even the Bible, have some good stuff to say, but just not about white folks.

Their Time Is Gonna Come

Judgment Day is coming, and like a blockbuster Hollywood movie, it will come to America first. According to the Nation of Islam, the white race is a genetically engineered species of pale-skinned devils created by mad scientist Yakub through a grafting process from the original black race on the island Patmos. His reasons for creating these melanin-challenged troublemakers are unknown, but both Fard and Muhammad prophesied the white devils would rule for 6,000 years (starting in 1914), and then, it's *go time*. A fiery Armageddon will allow the true progenitors of earth to reclaim world dominance.

The Mother Plane

Though it *appears* that Elijah Muhammad died in 1975, NOI believers maintain instead that he escaped an assassination attempt and now spends his days flying through the sky, with copilot Fard, in the "Mother Plane," a wheel-shaped contraption that white Americans are said to mistake for a UFO. Purportedly built in Japan at a cost of $15 billion, it was constructed of a super-strength steel whose composition is still unknown. There are 1,500 small wheels within the Mother Plane, each of which carries three bombs that will be used during Armageddon to destroy undesirables (guess who). If you have never seen the Mother Plane, or have only seen fictional accounts of such "UFOs" in movies or on TV, it's because that's white America's plan to discredit the Mother Plane's authenticity. Gotcha!

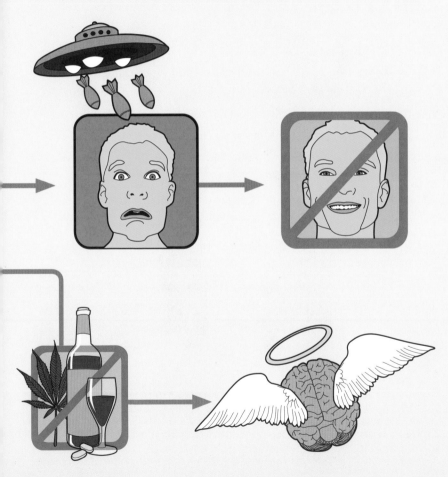

Rastafari Movement

The Rastafari Movement (or Rasta) gives new meaning to the term "heaven on earth," not only by endorsing reggae music, healthy food, not shampooing, and regular toking of the *ganja* as holy rituals, but also by delivering what few other religions can: true immortality. For those of you impatient for the Second Coming to arrive, there's no need to fret: It already happened for the Rastas, in the form of Ethiopian leader Haile Selassie. This former African emperor is regarded as *Jah*, God incarnate. His to-do list includes ushering in Judgment Day, when he will summon home the virtuous to Mount Zion (Africa/Ethiopia) to live forever—just as the song says—in peace, love, and understanding. Many Rastas consider themselves the true Israelites and Selassie a reincarnation of Jesus. According to some traditions, Selassie was number 225 in an unbroken chain of Ethiopian monarchs that originated with King Solomon and the Queen of Sheba.

The Kind Bud

Rastas do like the ganja, and use it for ceremonial purposes as specified in the Holy Book itself (Genesis 1:12). (Not sure this argument would work with Mom or Dad, but, hey, it's worth a shot.) For Rastas, smoking the kind bud is a spiritual act bringing them closer to Jah. And that little issue of its illegality? It's not surprisin', mon, that Babylon would want to put a stop to the opening of minds. Specifically, Rastas take part in ceremonies called "reasonings," reminiscent of late-night college dorm room sessions, where participants gather, smoke out, and discuss political and social issues. The livelier *binghi* ceremony is marked by days of singing, dancing, feasting, and of course, smoking the ganja. Ready to sign up?

Buffalo Soldier

Bob Marley is perhaps the most famous Rasta, and his music is responsible for the international growth of the Rasta movement. Reggae is viewed as an important channel for conveying the Rasta religion to a broad audience—the music is the message. Other than reggae and the Bible (specifically, the New Testament Book of Revelations; according to the Rastaman, it's all 'der, mon), Rasta prides itself on having no central organizational body, no edifices of worship (many see their bodies as the only necessary temple), and no singular holy text.

Babylon by Bus

Rastafarians do not generally believe in an afterlife but do believe that a chosen few, or true Rastas, are immortal—not just everlasting but *everliving*. The down side is that, by extension, there is no heaven as it is commonly conceived. Instead, Rastas look to Zion, or Africa, and, more specifically, to Ethiopia as heaven on earth. Now, if you are white, you can *technically* become a member of this Jamaican-born movement, but you should know your race makes you part of Babylon, the Rastas' term for the much-disdained oppressive, modern world. Consequently, the expectation of everliving life for you, pale skin, might be a tad optimistic.

Roman Catholicism

It takes a while for a body to decompose, but impatient types can find solace in the fact that the Catholic God works faster than bacteria. Upon death your soul goes right on up for the reckoning—no waiting—which many find appealing. In addition, there are other attractions: The Church goes heavy on the ritual and features plenty of goth fetishism, plus you can be forgiven for a whole lot on earth should you confess and ask for absolution. And for those who like to be part of the cool crowd, the Catholic Church is a total PR machine; you can't argue that, good or bad, St. Peter's little start-up hasn't dominated the headlines for centuries.

However, folks who behave badly and don't repent will have every shortcoming tallied up before their very eyes. Should you be condemned to hell—not a particularly attractive choice—not even the Second Coming will spring you: Eternal torment is your only option. As a Catholic, you started off at birth behind the eight ball, as all humans have been doomed since Eve first took a spin with some bad fruit.

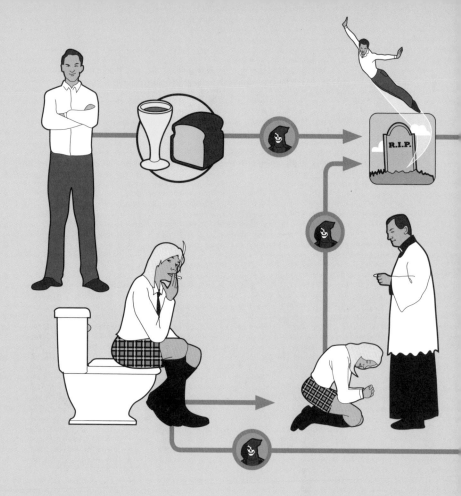

Getting There

According to Matthew, heaven is reserved for those whose love for God has been perfected in this life, which is not as easy as it sounds. If you want some CliffsNotes™ on how to fast-track, consider the sacraments of the catechism, which include baptism, confirmation, Eucharist, penance, anointing of the sick, holy orders, and matrimony. Though matrimony may sound like the simplest requirement (certainly easier than priesthood), birth control is *verboten* so you will need to practice some systematic abstinence if you don't want to spring for an extended van. Penance, therefore, might be what saves you from your sins (you do actually have to feel sorry for what you did). Depending on your priest, absolution could come by way of saying a few Hail Marys or buying the church a new roof, depending on just how bad you were.

Option A: Heaven

Though conventional wisdom says that some regular confession will get you a ticket to heaven, chances are you're less than likely to pass through the pearly gates on the first try. When you do, if you do, you'll find good, pious company in the eternal realm. In fact, Roman Catholics believe that God's main heavy, Michael the Archangel, will spirit your soul up to meet St. Peter at the entrance, where he will deliver what is termed "particular judgment" in allowing you inside or sending you down to purgatory to wait for a spot to open up. Think of it as the mother of all condo associations, and Peter's the only one who's got the keys.

Option B: Purgatory

Those of you just shy of perfect love will get a time-out of sorts to think over your shortcomings and sinful ways. Your visit is determined by your deeds; sin a lot, and you might as well settle in. You can leave your mittens at home—the fire of purgatory is hot enough to cleanse you of your residual sin, given time. Cool your heels with visions of clouds and angels and, if you lived an Amy Winehouse kind of life, pray for the Final Judgment to spring you a little faster.

Option C: Eternal Hellfire

You've been bad. Very bad. Did a little stem-cell research? Needed an exorcism but couldn't find the time? Did the devil make you do it? Whatever the reason, be prepared, because the hell option ain't pretty. Think of a never-ending blind date with someone both ugly and boring. It's worse than that. And the really bad news, not even the Second Coming can save you.

The Rosicrucian Fellowship

Fans of *The Da Vinci Code*, look out: The Rosicrucian Fellowship is tailor-made for you! Secret brotherhoods, different planes of existence, and a complex system of cosmic cycles involving not just evolution but spiritual *involution*—do you need to know more? You can. In fact, Rosicrucian Fellowship (also called the International Association of Christian Mystics) ideas are practiced correspondence-style, based on founder Max Heindel's texts, including the preeminent *Rosicrucian Cosmo-Conception*. You can rest easy knowing that the Fellowship is here to help as you pore through impenetrable materials with the goal of accepting Christian principles through esoteric study. These are a brainy bunch with a penchant for sci-fi (just like the folks at Microsoft), with a lot of metaphysical terms at once strangely compelling and completely inscrutable—*life waves, virgin spirits, seed atoms*. Just take your time and study your lessons, and perhaps you'll catch on.

The Three E's

The basic gist is nice and simple: All humans get multiple shots at material existence in order to equal-ize human experience and, hence, the chance to transcend rebirth. After all, as the Fellowship reasons, someone born into the slums will probably make different choices than someone born to a well-off family with good values (if this is not an oxymoron). So why should Slum Boy be punished, while Mr. Harvard gets off scot-free for doing what only came natural given his opportunity and education? The cycle of rebirth, they postulate, serves not to punish bad behavior, but to educate, elucidate, and equalize.

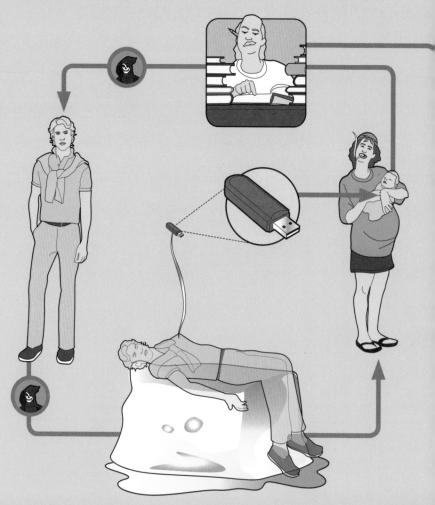

Transfer Complete

The moment of death is described by the Fellowship really as a birth, including umbilical imagery in which the Spirit pulls in your etheric (or vital) and physical bodies by a slender silver cord. As the ego is released, your astral body (your soul) takes with it a "seed atom," which has been stored during your lifetime in your heart's left ventricle (which explains that shadow on your MRI). This seed atom, like a tiny microchip on to which your life experiences have been imprinted, is moved, following death, from your etheric body into your astral body. Perhaps the most disturbing part of this scenario is that you're not really dead until that data transfer from your "essence" to your soul is complete, and it can take up to eighty-four hours (depending on your connection speed). During that time, you can still feel pain, making embalming and burial unpleasant, and cremation, well . . . you can imagine. Understandably, Members of the Fellowship ask to be placed on ice during these eighty-four hours following release from their physical bodies, so the transfer can occur peacefully and without pain ("release" forms are available online).

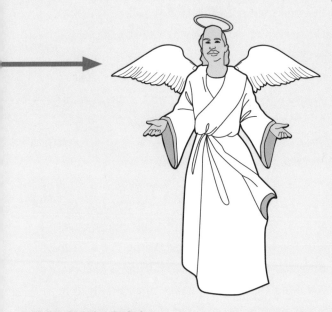

Involution, Evolution, Confusion

There are seven worlds that make up the lowest of the seven Cosmic Planes, each with its own rate of vibration and density. It helps to suspend your perceptions of time and space here, as the Worlds and the Cosmic Planes do not form a hierarchical structure, but permeate one another with no limits or boundaries (think: lava lamp). Evolving virgin spirits must pass through five of these worlds in order to manifest as human and then become godlike, through a process called "evolution." The attainment of self-consciousness so that you can manifest as a material being in the first place is called "involution." Confused? Now you know why you have to study.

Santeria

While Vodou is big in Haiti and parts of the South, the epicenter of Santeria—a Yoruban-Catholic combo—is Cuba and Brazil, where Spanish colonists baptized newly captured Nigerian slaves involuntarily upon their arrival. Not in the most advantageous of bargaining positions, the slaves devised an ingenious method for keeping their religion alive and making whitey happy at the same time. They simply equated each of their *orishas* (or powerful spirits and emanations of God) with a corresponding Catholic saint. (For instance, Babalz Ayi, orisha of the sick, is replaced with St. Lazarus, patron of the sick; St. Barbara, patron of lightning, thunder, and fire is subbed for Chango, ruler of thunder, lightning, and fire.) Santeria's teachings and rituals are passed on only orally to inductees, a practice that has no doubt contributed to some of the bad PR this religion has received over the years. Yes, followers do take part in a little animal sacrifice here and there, but c'mon, it's just a *chicken*, and they swear the deed is done humanely. They break from Catholic tradition, too, by drawing a line at the Holy See's version of a fiery hell. (These folks have taken enough flak from the Catholics—do they have to suffer after death, too?) Instead, they substitute a pleasantly benign reincarnation scenario that offers solace and peace.

Who's Your Daddy?

Santeria devotees believe that humans continually move between the invisible and visible worlds. After a bit of rest and rejuvenation in heaven, the departed soul is reincarnated, generally as the child of its original offspring. (So be nice to your kids and grandkids, because they might be deciding how much TV *you* get to watch.) The better you were in the last life, the more choice you have in deciding your fate in the next one. You also get some say in how long you stay in heaven before being reborn. It seems that all that blissful peace must get a little dull, judging by the number of souls reborn to this more-bittersweet realm, sometimes just months after death. As an interesting little twist on reincarnation, in Santeria it is possible to have multiple souls. So you can exist in both the visible and invisible realm simultaneously—literally, the best of both worlds.

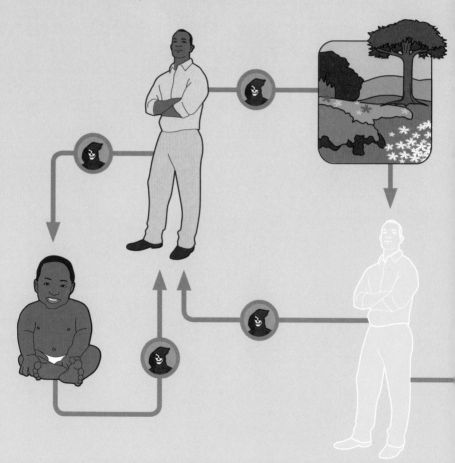

Dinner and a Show

Though the envisioned afterlife lacks the dramatic dichotomies of many faiths, let it not be said these folks are dull. Santeria employs show-stopping traditions like trance possession, animal sacrifice, and feverish drumming and dancing. The orishas are a demanding lot, you see, and they need food (thus the sacrifice), praise, and apparently some good entertainment to keep up their strength and spirits. Drama-seekers who aren't squeamish about bloodshed will find Santeria does not disappoint.

Make That a Skinny Latte, No Foam

Ancestor worship is a key component of Santeria. The dead are dependent upon the care and attentions of the living family so they don't lose strength and energy (and do what, *die?*). The dead are also critical conduits to the orishas and their supernatural power. Yet like Hollywood PR agents, these handlers for the orishas peddle their influence, making the orishas as hard to reach as Sean Penn. It is within the power of the dead to choose whether to harass or to protect the living, so keeping them on your good side is in your best interest. Inside tip: Two favorite offerings include animal blood (which fortifies them) and coffee (a sign of love and respect).

Scientology

If you harbor fantasies of hanging out in the hereafter with such celebs as Tom Cruise, Kirstie Alley, Priscilla Presley, and John Travolta, Scientology may be for you. Founded by science-fiction writer L. Ron Hubbard, Scientology is less a religion and more a booming personal-growth program with a number of elements worthy of its founder's original calling. As an "applied religious philosophy," Hubbard defined Scientology as the "study of knowledge or truth," and addressed the rehabilitation and salvation of the human spirit through a kind of personal counseling dubbed "auditing." Performed by a church-approved auditor, the goal of this one-on-one, question-and-answer session is to target and annihilate "engrams," or mental masses, until the "Preclear" has confronted (often multiple times) these troubling memories that are holding him or her back from happiness.

Beam Me Up, Ron

Scientology isn't particularly focused on God or the afterlife. And, celebrity Scientologists aside, the reality (according to church doctrine) is you will probably be reborn again and again until you realize your true nature as a "Thetan," or a "Clear" and immortal being. And, dear muddled soul, Tom and Kirstie are probably a lot closer to this eventuality than you are.

Contestant for Top-Five Creation Stories of All Time

Hubbard posited that around seventy-five million years ago, galactic ruler Xenu had a bad day and decided to bring billions of people to planet Earth. Then, for reasons not fully explained, he stacked them around volcanoes and proceeded to blow them up with hydrogen bombs. Their souls lingered, however, and have gathered around us like extraterrestrial ticks, causing all kinds of spiritual damage. This unfortunate event is referred to as either "Incident II" or "The Wall of Fire."

To add insult to injury, Xenu also purportedly trapped these Thetan souls and took them out to the movies. The films he showed them were meant to brainwash, rendering them too dense to return to their home planets. This episode is known as the "R6 implant," and, according to Hubbard, is why we have Christianity and a belief in heaven, hell, and other crazy notions. Wow.

Operating Thetan

Auditing plays out more like an intervention than a Catholic mass. The auditor employs a specially designed (and right out of *The Twilight Zone*) electro-psychometer to aid in locating the areas of spiritual distress. You are rated on a tone scale, from -40 (Total Failure) to +40 (Serenity of Being). Those who score very high are said to be Clear, and achieve the level of "Operating Thetan." An OT has presumably dispatched all pre-birth, current life, and previous-life traumas, and is now free to exit the reincarnation loop, bypass the confines of the physical universe, and become one with God. Until then, resign yourself to some painful self-analysis and an unknown number of lives in order to get it right.

Seventh-Day Adventist

Seventh-Day Adventists are your basic conservative Christians, so why not become a Catholic or a good old Southern Baptist? Well, they don't have the promise of unconsciousness instead of death, nor a rank-breaking Saturday Sabbath, do they?

The Seventh-Day Adventists have been awaiting the Day of Judgment for quite a while. The first prophecy emanated from farmer William Miller. It was revealed to him that God would do some housecleaning "unto 2,300 days." Miller took that to mean years instead, starting in 457 BCE (of course!). A little number crunching put the Reckoning sometime between March 21, 1843, and March 21, 1844. Well, it didn't happen. So a follower of Miller reconfigured the numbers and pushed the date back to October 22, 1844. That didn't happen either. Many followers left the movement then; those who remained became known as the Adventists, buoyed by the technicality found by Ellen White. The original prophecies, she claimed, weren't wrong, but referred instead to the advent of the "Investigative Judgment," a time when Jesus was consumed with background checks and would follow shortly with his return. Still waiting. Any day now.

BFF

According to Adventists, God is your buddy. And you spend time with him like all friends do, you tell him what's happening in your life, you share a laugh, you snuggle with him. You're even in God's family photo album. And you're not alone: Adventists, exhibiting a Colors-of-Benetton type philosophy, remind their membership that even the Buddha-loving Nepalese and shamanistic Yupiks are featured there.

Don't Hit the Snooze Button

After death, however, God seems to get a bit less chummy with some of his "buddies." Those Nepalese and Yupiks, unless they see the light and become Christian, will probably not be hanging with God for too much longer.

According to Adventist doctrine, when you die—no matter your religion—you enter a state of unconsciousness until the Second Coming, when Jesus will issue a wake-up call to the righteous, both living and dead. The rest get to sleep in . . . for another thousand years during which Jesus has a lot of paperwork to catch up on. He spends this millennium judging the sins of the late sleepers, consigning a now desolate Earth to Satan and his band of merrymakers.

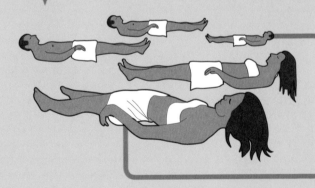

Feel the Burn

At the close of the thousand years, Jesus comes down again, and if you don't make this second cut you (along with new buddy Satan) burn up on the spot in an all-consuming fire. Then there will be a new Earth cleansed of all those pesky sinners and others who do not think the way you do. What a relief! Do you feel God's love now? No eternal fire and brimstone, just simple, clean annihilation.

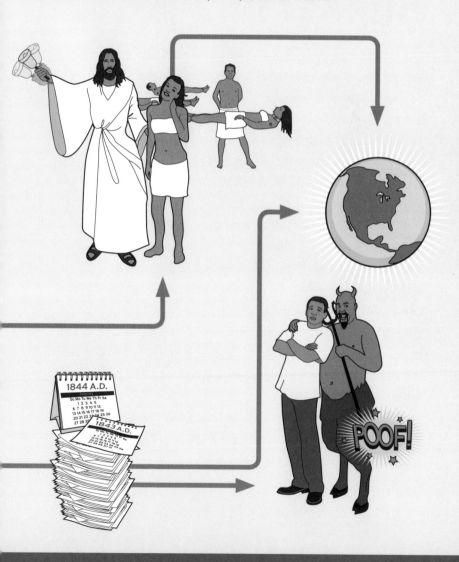

Shakers

The Shakers are looking for a few good men, and women (they are nothing if not egalitarian). Well, actually more than a few. You see, only four members of this Protestant offshoot are left in the *world,* and two are getting on in years. What are the perks, you ask? A quaint, rural Maine village to call home, some handy woodworking skills, and a quiet and peaceful life of austere pleasures. The drawbacks? Well, you can never have sex again, for one. That's right, the Shakers insist on celibacy for all members. Thus the problem with their membership numbers. However, despite this obvious organizational flaw, the Shakers have actually hung in there. The United Society in Christ's Second Appearing, the sect's original name, was founded by Ann Lee in 1747 in Manchester, England. Persecuted for such radical beliefs as pacifism and racial and gender equality, the group hightailed it to the New World. Shaker popularity peaked during the Civil War, with upward of 5,000 members. (The Shakers' status as the nation's first official conscientious objectors probably helped boost the rolls.) As the early twentieth century issued in a new age of prosperity and modernity, the group saw their numbers significantly dwindle.

If I Had a Hammer

Unlike in traditional Christianity, heaven on earth is a main Shaker objective. This goal is manifest in the careful planning and running of their villages. Physical work is viewed as a form of worship, with obviously good results. Shaker design and craftsmanship is renowned. Other major tenets include the aforementioned celibacy, regular confession of sin (before witnesses), and pacifism. The Shakers live a communal existence as well, and are barred from owning any personal property. All activities, from buying a new toothbrush to taking a trip into town, must be okayed by the group. Even in death the idea of individuality is eschewed: In the late 1800s the Sabbathday Lake community, home to the last remaining Shakers, removed all the tombstones from their graveyard and inserted a lone marker inscribed with a single word: *Shakers.*

Taking Conversion to a New Level

As for the afterlife, in keeping with their ascetic M.O., Shakers embellish very little on their vision of the hereafter. Adhering to their Protestant roots, the Shakers hold to a basic notion of heaven and hell consistent with the larger Christian Church. Spiritualism also influenced the Shakers' view of life after death. Mother Ann, the group's founder, was reportedly visited many times by spirits who revealed the Gospel to her, which she in turn passed on to other members. In the years following her death, members of several New England Shaker villages reported visitations from the dead as well. They claimed these ghosts, some of them famous people, not only came to visit but stayed—possessing the bodies of some of the community's Brothers and Sisters. These ghostly squatters were then counseled by Shaker Elders, brought into line, and then handily converted. (That's one way to get new members!)

Shinto

Are you that wavering agnostic who hangs on just for a little insurance in the afterlife? Then jump on the Shinto bandwagon! The official religion of Japan doesn't recognize any formal hierarchy of deities or single god (no religious royalty here). Instead, life revolves around the appeasement and worship of *kami*, spirits that take many forms, from physical manifestations, such as plum trees, to what might be considered a collective pooling of soulness (so Japanese). Shinto was forged mostly from a creation story that describes the birth of Japan, featuring the sun goddess Amaterasu, who created the world. Amaterasu is considered a kami, but isn't really afforded special kami status, save that she is reputed to be the mother of all Japanese emperors, who thus live as *ikigami*, or "living kami." Though a case could be made that the president of the United States is more than a little full of himself, following World War II the Allies got sanctimonious about Emperor Hirohito claiming kami status, maybe worried about a literal god complex. He was made to denounce his claim to divinity.

I Am a Rock

The term *kami* refers to an incredible variety of impish spirits and even natural essences. They can be found inhabiting natural geographic features such as lakes, rivers, rice paddies, and unusual rocks. The collective group of kami is referred to as *yaoyorozu no kami,* literally translated as "eight million kami." Bigwig kami are afforded their own shrines, which people visit to make offerings or to petition forgiveness, but most kami are not represented as deities with human attributes (some modern Shinto priests have made a move to anthropomorphize the kami a bit more). Instead, all kami are said to possess both gentle (*nigi-mitama*) and aggressive (*ara-mitama*) souls. Depending on which soul is in control, a kami can cause unpredictable, even unpleasant, events, like lightning, floods, or spewing volcanoes.

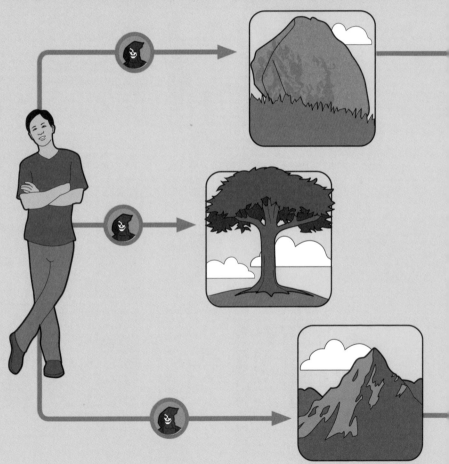

We Are Family

As soon as a baby is born in Japan, his or her name is automatically recorded at a Shinto shrine—regardless of the parents' consent, or religion. The girl or boy is designated a "family child," or *ujiko*, and, upon death, becomes a "family spirit," or *ujigami*. In keeping with the family theme, as an ujigami you don't retain your individual soulness, or *tama*, but instead are subsumed into your ancestral kami-at-large.

After death, your kin will regularly honor you with rice, fish, and pickles (if you're lucky), at the family shrine. It is said that kami respond to truthful prayers, so it pays to keep your kami happy and satisfied.

He's a Kami, I'm a Kami, Wouldn't You Like to Be a Kami, Too?

Regardless of your comportment on earth, when you die, you also become a kami. Automatically! In general, Shinto supports the, well, lazy. You need not have prayed, sacrificed, been baptized, or anything else to ensure a smooth passing. In fact, you don't even have to be a Shintoist to reap the benefits of this mellow, animist faith (though you may need to relocate).

Sikhism

Sikhism isn't just a religion, it's a look. A *badass* look. It's not just the *dastar*, or turban, that all Sikh men must wear (for women it's optional) as a sign of dignity, but also the *kirpan*, a ceremonial sword carried at all times to symbolize your fight against injustice. On this and many other levels, Guru Nanak Dev got it right when he founded Sikhism in 1469, not, as is commonly believed, as an offshoot of Islam or Hinduism, but as a separate belief system. Whether it's the sword, the theology, or the break Sikhs get from wearing helmets on their motor-cycles (because of the dastar), something seems to resonate—Sikhism is the fifth-largest religion in the world.

In its own way, Sikhism is like the perfect man—attractive, strong, and sensitive. All good Sikhs adhere to a strict code of conduct that includes rejecting the caste system, practicing re-ligious tolerance, and maintaining absolute equality for women.

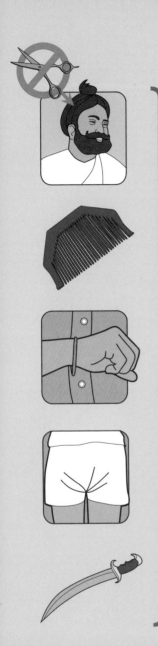

What to Wear

Sikhism is focused on freeing you from the cycle of reincarnation and getting you to commune directly with God. To do so you must follow the five Physical Articles of Faith, or the five K's. *Kesh* is unshorn hair (hidden under your dastar); *kanga* is a wooden comb, worn under the dastar, used to keep your locks tidy and to represent self-discipline; *kara* is an iron bracelet worn to remind you of your bond with God; *kaccha* are Sikh boxers (as in undies) worn to remind you of restraint (i.e., keep them on); and finally, that totally rightous *kirpan*.

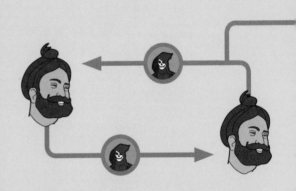

The Four Stages of Sikhdom

There are four stages of a Sikh's spiritual evolution, starting on the ground floor and ending with Gurmukh, as close to heaven as the Sikhs get, embodying what others might call "total enlightenment."

Stage One: Manmukh

You have much to learn, grasshopper. Stage One probably includes most of the people you know—self-centered and focused on the material world. If you can get over your addiction to the five cardinal vices—lust, anger, greed, attachment, and pride—you can start moving down that pathway toward salvation. The good news: Sikhs think a "healthy" family life is all *good*. Lust may be bad, but celibacy's just not normal.

Stage Two: Sikh

So, you've made the first step on to the path of learning. Congrats. Make sure you adhere to the official code of conduct *(Reht Maryada)* and you'll do just fine. Sure, you can't drink anymore, and you'll need to toss those Marlboros in the trash, but doing *seva* (community service) and honest labor isn't the worst way to spend your time. An extra incentive to get through this stage: At the next level you get to trade in your last name for something a little more regal: All male Khalsa add "Singh" after their last name (which means "lion"), while all female Khalsa add "Kaur" after theirs (meaning "prince"–not "princess"!). All Sikhs are expected to be on the path to Khalsa, so keep motivated.

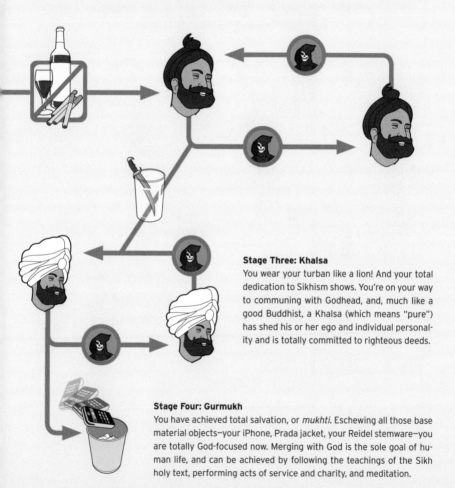

Stage Three: Khalsa

You wear your turban like a lion! And your total dedication to Sikhism shows. You're on your way to communing with Godhead, and, much like a good Buddhist, a Khalsa (which means "pure") has shed his or her ego and individual personality and is totally committed to righteous deeds.

Stage Four: Gurmukh

You have achieved total salvation, or *mukhti*. Eschewing all those base material objects–your iPhone, Prada jacket, your Reidel stemware–you are totally God-focused now. Merging with God is the sole goal of human life, and can be achieved by following the teachings of the Sikh holy text, performing acts of service and charity, and meditation.

Snake-handling Pentacostalism

Participation in this group of crazy-talking, teetotaling Appalachian literalists might not give you any more options after death than mainstream Christianity does, but it sure fast-tracks you there. It could be argued that the adherents of snake-handling Pentecostalism didn't do so good in English class, seeing as how they interpret the biblical quote from Mark 16:17-18, "they shall take up serpents," as a good idea, rather than a metaphor. This literal reading stems from their belief in biblical inerrancy, the theory that every word of the Bible is absolute fact. In addition to fondling venomous rattlers and copperheads, some snake-handling Pentecostals also take up another biblical passage as admonition and quaff poison like frat boys at a kegger. As with the snakes, followers count on his Holiness to protect them from any danger stemming from ignoring Mr. Yuk. They also share one of the Pentecostals' more infamous rituals, that of glossolalia, or speaking in tongues.

This Party Ain't No Rave

If you're looking for a good time, seek danger elsewhere. Followers obey rigid (and dowdy) dress codes and shun movies. Tobacco and alcohol—except that laced with strychnine—are strictly *verboten*. Jesus-lovers not into smooching with serpents, and looking for a little more latitude on the fun spectrum, may want to check out the closely aligned Charismatic movement, similar in theology but with less risk.

Get Thee to Jesus

The nice thing about the aforementioned biblical inerrancy, one would think, would be having a concrete, literal roadmap to heaven, the fluffy, benign, and tastefully decorated realm beyond those pearly gates into which most Christians buy. But most of the snake-handling Pentacostals require speaking in tongues as a sign of salvation. It's this emphasis on the Holy Spirit working within your body (indeed, snake-handling Pentacostals often meet in private homes and shun formal churches) that separates this group so fundamentally from other evangelical Christians. Speaking in tongues, a "dry" baptism of sorts by the Holy Ghost, is possible after Sanctification, a process in which all your past sins are cast away, as is your wicked nature and even your tendency toward sin.

Wear Your Mouth Guard

And should you not repent? Suffice it to say, hell involves the fairly strict interpretation of biblical passages that include the words "eternal," "condemnation," "wailing," and "gnashing of teeth." That can't be good. On the other hand, it doesn't sound so different from a five-hour religious service in which participants scream, cry, and writhe on the floor as they receive the Holy Spirit or are bitten by snakes and poisoned. It's all in the eye of the beholder.

Spiritualism

Cynics take note: Not only is there life after death, but members of the Spiritualism movement (sometimes called Spiritism) say they can prove it. Adherents (Sir Arthur Conan Doyle and Elizabeth Barrett Browning were early followers) claim that the scientific proof comes from their direct communication with spirits of the deceased via mediumship (séances and Ouija boards and stuff). This movement's connection to Christianity is tangential at best. While some of the original followers were radical Quakers (an incongruous thought in itself), Spiritualists do not buy into the Bible as the primary source on the hereafter, but instead look to their own direct experience with the dead. Instead of believing in heaven, hell, the Resurrection, or the Day of Judgment, Spiritualism postulates that the soul progresses through a number of spiritual realms via transmigration. While there are contemporary Spiritualists—and a pop-culture infatuation with the practice that just won't quit—this movement hit its high-water mark in the period from 1840 to 1930.

Trading Up

Spiritualists believe there are seven realms. The human soul is composed of an ethereal matter that leaves the physical body at death but continues to linger around the earthly plane for a while in one of several realms, depending on whether you've been naughty or nice.

The bad seeds are destined initially for the **First Realm** (aka the "lower astral realm"), which is the closest the Spiritualists get to hell or purgatory. It can take a while for a soul to make amends for misdeeds and be upgraded to a higher realm (known officially as the Law of Progress).

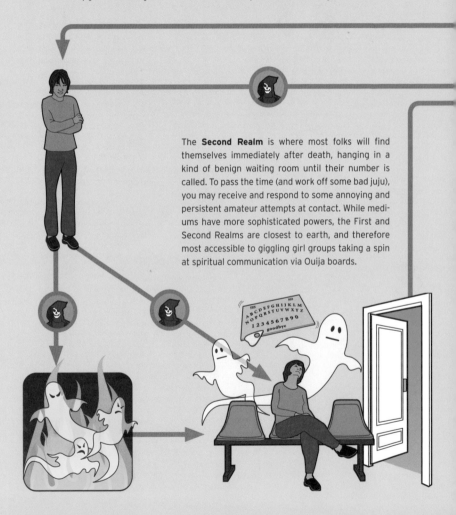

The **Second Realm** is where most folks will find themselves immediately after death, hanging in a kind of benign waiting room until their number is called. To pass the time (and work off some bad juju), you may receive and respond to some annoying and persistent amateur attempts at contact. While mediums have more sophisticated powers, the First and Second Realms are closest to earth, and therefore most accessible to giggling girl groups taking a spin at spiritual communication via Ouija boards.

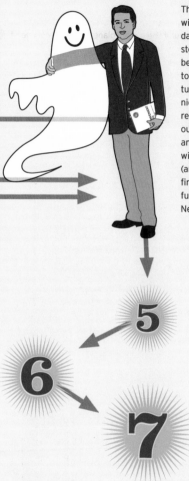

The **Third Realm** is where the best of your earthly brethren will end up (that girl at work who remembers everyone's birthday, the folks who always bring their own bag to the grocery store, Nobel Peace Prize winners, and the like). It is generally believed that from this Third Realm, souls can decide whether to be reincarnated or to bypass that option for loftier spiritual locales. Experienced mediums are often in clear communication with the goody-two-shoes types found here, as this realm is light and bright, and communication channels with our world are still open. As Third Realmers acquire knowledge and moral fortitude (in some cases, through their dealings with the living), they may choose to progress to the higher (and presumably harder to dial into) **Fourth, Fifth, Sixth,** and finally **Seventh Realms.** Each successive level is more beautiful and offers better conditions, like trading up your cramped New York apartment for a Brooklyn brownstone.

Spiritual Self-Improvement 101

Spiritualists believe that the personality of the deceased (pets included) continues in a new spiritual body after death, as do all our memories. Therefore, death itself is not stagnant but allows for, and even encourages, personal growth. For those of you who thought that, at the very least, death would mark the end of the tiresome task of bettering yourself, think again. While it no doubt signals an end to the pursuit of physical goals, like fitting into a size-six dress, it doesn't mean the end of moral and intellectual improvement.

Talking Points

Communication with the dead in these other realms is facilitated by a variety of means, most commonly by the services of mediums, those endowed with special telepathic powers who can bridge the divide between our world and others. Why bother checking in with the dead, you ask? Well, while these lingering spirits may be haunted by some of their own unresolved issues (depending on the realm they reside in), they are still closer to God than you are, and thus may be able to provide advice and guidance—like whether Tommy from science class *likes* you, or whether your dead grandmother is mad at you for wearing her brooch.

The Twelve Tribes

Members of the Twelve Tribes believe fundamentally in two tenets—the first, that God gave all humans instinctive knowledge of good and evil, and the second that in the end God will judge you fairly, according to how well you obeyed your conscience during your lifetime. Add to that a communal lifestyle, Israeli folk dancing, homeschooling, and some controversial feelings about Jews, and hey, you've got a new religion. Basically an offshoot of Christian fundamentalism, the Twelve Tribes differs in some significant ways, the most distinctive of which is that it adds a third option on to heaven and hell.

Experience waiting tables or pulling espresso shots is not required, but could come in handy should you choose to get right with God, Twelve Tribes-style. Tribe members live in collective communities often funded by operating restaurants, in much the way founder Elbert Eugene Spriggs and his wife, Marsha, supported their first intentional community with a coffee shop in Tennessee—eventually starting both a new church and a new chain of Yellow Deli restaurants. That's entrepreneurship!

Sure, they've gotten in some hot water over child abuse (those charges didn't stick!), but if getting away from it all—by releasing all of your possessions, funds, and power—sounds liberating, perhaps the Tribes life, and afterlife, is for you.

The Ideal Scenario

You've dumped your IRA into the communal pot, burned all your porn, and have done your very best to stay pure in this dirty world and live as a disciple of Yahshua (Hebrew for "Jesus"). Well, it's not just your distinct hairstyle that will make you part of the Twelve Tribes "set apart," or Holy. Once you die, all that giving you've done on earth means a straight shot to God, where you will be hired as a universal ambassador for Yahshua, jetting about like Condee Rice through the Nations of God's Eternal Kingdom and helping your boss rule over the righteous.

Nation of Good Enough

Now, the Righteous may not have joined the community, given up all of their personal wealth, nor renounced no-no's like adultery and homosexuality like other Tribe members. But still, if you were basically a good person, feared God, and mostly did the right thing, your punishment is subject to term limits. After you pay for your sins, come Judgment Day you will be resurrected to one of the endless Nations of God's Eternal Kingdom where you get to while away the rest of your infinite days. The Nations are a bit like India in that the population keeps growing exponentially as more people are born, die, and are resurrected. When it becomes as crowded as Mumbai, members will get shuffled around to new Nations created just for that purpose.

You Dirty Pig

Oh, woe to the Unjust and the Filthy. For you, death promises nothing but an eternal cruise on a lake o' fire. Do not pass "GO," do not collect $200. You can expect no relief from the torment and torture *ever*.

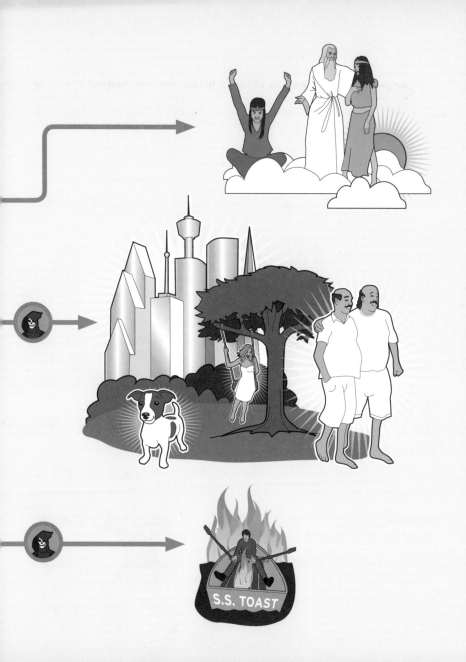

The Unification Church

The good news: The Messiah is among us! Belonging to one of the few religions to posit that the Second Coming has arrived, adherents of the Unification Church—whose followers are dubbed "Moonies"—believe they will create the Kingdom of Heaven on earth, but first, humans must create a pure race. According to Unification doctrine, Adam and Eve aren't the True Parents of humankind because Eve got a little something from Satan on the side, polluting the waters, so to speak. Jesus had a plan to undo their sin and create the pure children destined to inhabit the earth, but he was killed before he could marry and procreate. Fortunately, Unification founder Reverend Sun Myung Moon was born as the "third Adam." Not only have he and his wife managed to create no fewer than a dozen pure (sinless) children the old-fashioned way, he has figured out a way to purify you, too, should you submit to an arranged marriage with his blessings. In fact, Daddy has thought of everything, offering eternal salvation based on three attainable axes: accepting Moon as your True Father; being able to follow his impenetrable text, *Divine Principle*; and hating Communism.

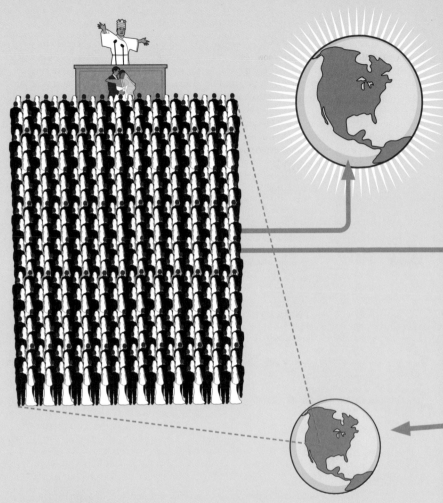

My Big Fat Moonie Wedding

If you've always dreamed of a big wedding, the first tenet—accepting Moon and his wife as your True Parents, and helping to create a pure race by becoming a True Parent yourself—should be right up your alley. Not only will Moon find you your perfect match, he'll plan your wedding (for a modest fee), where you and your betrothed and, oh, tens of thousands of other couples will all say, "I do." (The largest of such ceremonies reportedly involved 3.6 million couples via satellite.) Your physical redemption can also be achieved through a ritual known as "blood cleansing," whereby men have sex with women who have been "cleansed" by having sex with Moon himself. Oh, Daddy!

Pay It Down

Unification principles on the afterlife rely a great deal on a cooperative relationship between the living and the dead. Moonies follow what is known as the "Law of Indemnity" outlined in *Divine Principle*, which dictates that all of God's children must pay down at least part of their sin in order to achieve salvation. While alive, you can accomplish this through fasting, recruiting others into the Church, or just by spending cash, either on behalf of your own soul or to help someone else who is already dead and hasn't quite made it to paradise. Objects imbued with special powers of indemnification—including vases and vessels—are available for sale for this very purpose. Does it work? You'll have to wait until death to find out, but the courts are weighing in with a "no." (A $150-million settlement was made to former members of Japan's Unification Church who claimed they were forced to purchase these sacred objects, "faith" and "proof" being mutually exclusive.)

Spirit Buddies

Should you die before the Kingdom of Heaven on earth has been achieved, you will ascend to some part of the spirit world, depending on both how much sin you have paid off and your actions on earth. In keeping with a philosophy transmitted via a living Messiah, paradise doesn't look much different from day-to-day life and includes the same likes, dislikes, and goals as you had before death. Spirits in good standing operate much like guardian angels, guiding their chosen human counterparts toward good deeds. Less pristine souls may choose to pay down their own debt of sin (and help their earthly counterparts do the same) by "testing" humans or meting out punishment, like a karmic spirit mafia. Moon never bothered himself much with hell, believing that, unlike Jesus, he will succeed in expanding heaven, rendering the devil's lair inconsequential.

Universal Sufism

Though Sufism translates as "the Way of the Pure" and has roots in austere eighth-century Islam, modern Universal Sufism is more of a tolerant and embracing sort of religion. Borrowing a bit from Buddhism, Hinduism, and Gnosticism, in addition to Islam, this metaphysical self-improvement-program-cum-religion facilitates your ascension to the Divine Light through self-knowledge. In fact, besides being kick-ass poets and good (and fast!) dancers, Sufis offer some refreshing self-determination over your own spiritual destiny that might tempt you into becoming a whirling dervish, too. After you die, instead of standing looking all hangdog in front of God waiting for the grand pronouncement, you judge your actions, thereby bringing about your own heaven or hell. (But, c'mon, who's really going to send themselves to *hell?*)

Universal Sufism founder Hazrat Inayat Khan described the soul in metaphorical terms as a tree, in that the same animating force in the trunk also lengthens the branches and grows the leaves and seeds. Sufis also describe the soul as the "Universal Intelligence" nabbed, like a fish in a net, by the body and the mind.

You've Got One Chance

Heaven and hell are not places but simply individual creations of individual minds. Heaven is equivalent to peace realized by the individual, while hell doesn't include fire as much as ignorance. (Your prayers have been answered! George Bush is in hell!) And it is recognized that because this is all based on the individual, your hell just might be someone else's heaven, like watching golf on TV. Heaven and hell are the results of individual actions in lieu of destinations. Because your soul is not an everlasting nor separate entity, Sufis don't get behind the whole wheel-of-life through reincarnation thing, but instead aim to get it right the first time, in one lifetime.

The Astral Dome

Instead of karma, Sufis have the Law of Reciprocity, basically a stricter version of "do unto others." Reciprocity is envisioned as a dome, with good echoes coming back from good sounds, and earsplitting echoes returning from evil emissions. As Sufis shun absolutes, ultimately good and evil are up to you to decide and are dependent on the context and situation (like lying to your girlfriend if she asks if she's fat).

Vodou

Animal sacrifice, zombification, and voodoo-doll shenanigans have been long linked in the popular imagination with the practice of Vodou. In reality, this Afro-Caribbean faith, a combination of Western African beliefs and Catholicism, is a rather upbeat religion that places great importance on the power of spirits (who occasionally possess believers and force them to drink copious amounts of rum and engage in lewd and inappropriate behavior). Brought to the New World, Vodou later spread to the southern United States, specifically Louisiana, where a greater emphasis is placed on folk magic. Vodou features a rather extensive and colorful pantheon of gods and goddesses as well as one supreme creator, Gran Met. While acknowledged, Gran Met is considered too distant to be of much concern or the object of much direct worship. Instead, Voudouans, perhaps wisely, choose to keep the more immediate spirits (referred to en masse as the *loa*, or "mystery") happy. A particularly colorful example, the bawdy Baron Samedi sports a tux, a white top hat, and a foul mouth, and has a proclivity for rum and cigars. *The Baron made me do it, I swear.*

Mix Five Ingredients

Adherents of Vodou believe that the human being is composed of five essential ingredients: *n'ame*, *z'etolie*, *corps cadavre*, *gros bon ange*, and finally *ti bon ange*. The *corps cadavre* is the physical flesh and bone, *n'ame* is the vital energy essential for the body to function, the *z'etolie* is the particular individual's "star of destiny," and the soul is comprised of one part *ti bon ange* ("little guardian angel") and one part *gros bon ange* ("big guardian angel"). The *ti bon ange* is your personal soul, the essential element that makes you, you. This soul is vulnerable to damage or capture by evil when free of the body. And be warned, this includes not only the period after death but also during sleep or when under the possession of the loa during a ritual. The *gros bon ange*, on the other hand, enters the particular person at conception and is a part of the universal life energy that all living things share.

Repeat Sixteen Times

When the body dies, the soul remains near the corpse for seven days. During this week, the *ti bon ange* is most vulnerable to capture by a sorcerer who will make it into a "spiritual zombie" to do the evildoer's bidding. If you escape this fate, then the priest ritually severs your soul from your body, sending you to dwell in a place described rather ominously as the "dark waters" for a year and a day. Perhaps not your first choice for a soul sabbatical.

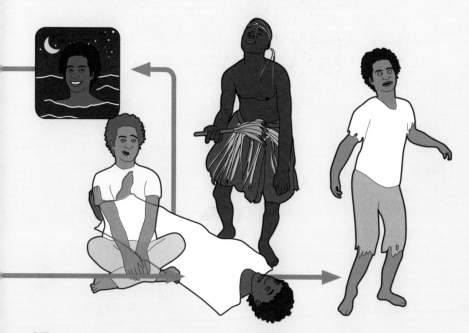

367

On day 367 after your death, family members raise your soul and deposit you into a *govi*, a red clay pot, to be fed, clothed, and (hopefully) treated like a god. In general, families are to treat these visiting ancestors like royalty. This might seem an optimistic expectation, but you know your own family best. At some designated future point (to the relief of your living relations), your soul is released from the govi and set free to live among the rocks and trees, awaiting rebirth.

Make it past these three hurdles, and your soul is home free. (In a sense; you have to go through sixteen total rebirths until you merge with the cosmic energy, meaning you have to successfully jump the spiritual zombie hoop a few more times.)

Wicca

If your idea of heaven is a week in Maui, get ready to join the coven and add Lughnasadh and Samhain to your already busy holiday calendar. Far from the black-pointy–hat-wearing, broomstick-wielding, poison-apple-pushing caricatures manifested in Technicolor, witches are simply followers of the Celts' ancient, duo-theistic (and gender-balanced), earth-worshipping religion far older than most of the world's established faiths. And though modern Wiccans have a range of afterlife beliefs, most revolve around reincarnation and a wondrous place called Summerland. If this sounds appealing to you, you are not alone; the Wiccan movement has experienced a kind of renaissance in the past ten years, with membership in the United States expanding nearly twentyfold.

Life Is Too Short

Wiccans believe that one life-time is not nearly enough to take in all the lessons of the universe; therefore, when you have absorbed all you can in your current incarnation, you die, retreating to Summerland to await redeployment in an appropriate body.

Three's a Charm (or Not)

Wiccans don't have a lot of rules, so for those of you averse to being told what to do, the Craft might be right up your alley. The central principle, or moral compass, of Wicca is belief in, and abiding of, the **Law of Threefold Return** (also known as karma). Wiccans believe that whatever you do, good or bad, will be revisited upon you not once or twice, but three times. Ouch. A sweet deal when helping old ladies across the street and buying Girl Scout cookies, but a decidedly worse scenario when cheating on your taxes or your husband. This notion of karma plays into the form of your reincarnated self as well. Really, it's all rather tidy and satisfying to contemplate. You were a greedy, self-serving Scrooge in this life. Well, in your next one you might be a poor beggar who is dependent on the kindness and generosity of others. That'll learn ya.

Soul Vacation

During your well-deserved breather in Summerland, your soul relaxes in a warm and sunny place (not surprisingly, this religion originated in the British Isles), complete with cool groves, clear streams, and lush, rolling hills. Your soul can visit with loved ones from past lives who happen to be Summerlanding at the same time. And if all of this paradise gets a little dull, never fear. Summerlanders are required to spend some time reviewing the accomplishments and failures of their past incarnation (like a country club, paradise has its price). Your process of self-improvement involves no judgment, no direct punishment (see Law of Threefold Return for details), just a gentle, though honest, review; a means by which your soul inches closer to perfection. Despite the pop-culture spin on witches hanging with the wrong crowd, there's no devil, nor hell, involved in Wicca—just pure Summerland (and a reincarnation reflective of your past deeds—for edification, of course). No wonder the Christians have mounted a smear campaign against these folks for so long. That's some stiff competition.

Beyond Summerland

So what happens when you have lived many lives, learned the lessons of the universe, and are itching for a promotion? Is there life after Summerland? Can you escape the reincarnation loop? Well, the Wiccans are understandably fuzzier on this point (after Summerland, who cares? Right?). It is generally agreed that reincarnation is the means by which the soul is perfected. And once you have lived in many varying conditions and thus learned all of your lessons, you will experience a final incarnation (as a Gandhi or Mother Teresa, say), and then move on to a higher plane. That is about as specific as the Wiccans get on this. Some describe it as nirvana, others as merging with the God/Goddess energy. Whatever it is, it's all good.

Yazdânism

So you don't want to be a member of any club that would have you? Then Yazdânism is for you, assuming you're an ethnic Kurd. It really is too bad that this pre-Islamic religion, otherwise known as the "Cult of Angels," frowns on outsiders crashing the party—because this *is* an afterlife party to die for. The Cult not only includes seven badass archangels that protect you while you're alive (from seven equally corrupting and malicious forces), but also has a high tolerance for other religions, a benign cycle of reincarnation, and no hell! If you're wondering where you sign up, the bad news is—you can't. As the story goes, the Kurdish Yazdâni are descendents of a baby boy born to Adam in a jar through a biological miracle (kind of like a sea monkey), while all other humans are the later progeny of both Adam *and* Eve, conceived after the whole who's-going-to-be-cursed-with-a-period thing got sorted out. Hence, no intermixing and no conversion. Sorry, but chances are you aren't going to sit with the cool kids on this one—you'll just have to listen to their conversation from the neighboring table. (Not surprisingly, the Yazdâni have long been the targets of Christian missionaries. *Jealous much?*)

The Magnificent Seven

Helping to keep you pumped up for the karmic cycle, the seven archangels for whom the religion is named (the Kurdish word *Yazdân* means "angel") will periodically join you by adopting human form, like heavenly drill sergeants jogging with their recruits. Melek Ta'us is the leader of the pack (he's also known as the Peacock Angel—it sounds tougher in Kurdish).

While the good angels dwell in what is termed heaven, this is a metaphorical concept rather than an actual place. There is no hell, conceptual or otherwise, it having been taken care of by Melek Ta'us long ago.

Speaking Metaphorically

The Cult brings no promise of eternal flame. In fact, acting as a sort of volunteer firefighter, the Peacock Angel saved up thousands of tears in jars for thousands of years until he had enough to extinguish the flames of hell, eradicating it forever. Just to keep you honest, the Yazdâni believe that your reward or punishment will be experienced as either misery, pain, and destitution, or success and health here on earth through your various incarnations. Vegetarian policemen might consider the Cult life hellish, however. In addition to not being allowed to marry or fraternize excessively with non-Yazdâni, you can't wear blue, eat lettuce, or spit.

Yazdâni's Little Black Book

All three branches of the Cult of Angels (Alevism, Yârsânism, and Yazidi) believe in the reincarnation of everlasting souls in animal, vegetable, or mineral form based on, yes, how you acted during your mortal spin. The pious pray at least twice a day toward Mosul, depending on the sect; follow the code of conduct outlined in their Arabic holy texts, usually translated as the "Book of Revelation" (or "Illumination") and the "Black Book"; and the Yazidi make a yearly pilgrimage to the tomb of Sheikh Adi to Lalish, a twelfth-century Sufi mystic they believe was the last incarnation of Archangel Melek Ta'us. Details on what makes you a good follower are scarce because the Cult keeps the rules a secret, probably to avoid further persecution by their Muslim neighbors.

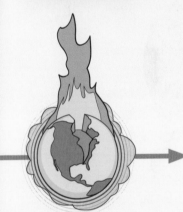

Toll Bridge

Things change up a bit with the Apocalypse, where righteous Kurds must pass God's judgment exam (a sort of cosmic tollbooth) in order to cross the bridge (*Perdivari*) and join with the Universal Spirit forever. Anything less than an A+ on your test gets you thrown into the universal incinerator, along with the rest of the planet.

Zoroastrianism

Do you lie awake at night, worrying that when you open your eyes, you may find yourself imprisoned in a casket, buried alive? Who doesn't? As a preventative measure, you may want to consider practicing Zoroastrianism, one of the oldest religions on the planet, whose customs dictate that upon death your body will be placed atop a roofless structure, called a "tower of silence," and left to the elements. If you're lucky enough to wake before the vultures get to you, you have an easy escape route. Don't you feel better?

Spawned by the teachings of the prophet Zoroaster (or Zarathustra), Zoroastrianism was the monotheistic "it" religion from the sixth century BCE until Islam kind of spoiled the party in 622 CE. It's still practiced in what was once called Persia, where Zoroastrians are sort of like Christian-prototype firebugs, revering all types of flame and holding fire sacred. Believers have free will to choose between evil and good, and fairly stock notions of heaven, hell, and the Resurrection to help keep you on the straight and narrow. Their motto sums it all up: *Good thoughts, good words, good deeds.*

Blind Date

Zoroastrians believe that, like a forlorn fawn standing by its dead mother, your babylike soul hovers near your still body for four days. On the morning of the fourth day, your soul finally separates and ascends to the *Chinvato-peretu*, the bridge that separates the physical world *(Geti)* from the spiritual one *(Minoi)*. There, you meet an "astral maiden" (or dude) called the *Kainini-Keherpa*, whose physical appearance reflects the content of your character. The previously pious and devoted are rewarded with a hottie, while the selfish and arrogant . . . *woof, woof, woof.*

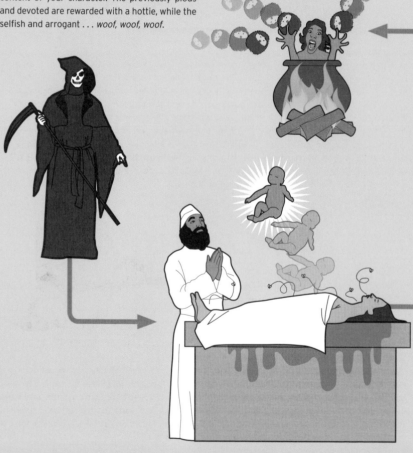

Judgment Day

Your astral date will accompany you to your judgment. Look to the specter on your arm for a clue as to whether you're headed toward the "abode of songs" (*Garodman*), where quite literally heaven awaits, or to *drujo-deman,* where you might guess what your other alternative looks like. If your imagination needs a little spark, you should know that many think Christianity's dark hell was an idea first spawned by the Zoroastrian *drujo-deman.* This grim destination is comprised of the *Dush-humat* (land of evil thoughts), *Dush-hukht* (evil words), *Dush-huvarsht* (evil deeds), and an unnamed pit of despair that makes the killer's basement in *Silence of the Lambs* seem like a spa. Holy texts describe punishments as wide-ranging as being dismembered, being cooked, having to eat your own corpse or the body and brains of your children, walking through molten metal, and, in a uniquely Zoroastrian twist, being bombarded by hedgehogs.

Tower of Silence

While you need not fear premortem internment, this is not a religion for those who require some post-mortem adoration. Zoroastrians believe that the impure body should not pollute the earth after death. Thus the dearly departed are abandoned to the elements and the vultures on their ceremonial towers, usually located on a mountain plateau. To add insult to injury, only *Nassesalars,* or special death lepers, may touch your lifeless body, which is bathed in cow urine before being left to decompose. Basically, you're the epitome of *ick.* But hey, you're dead. What do you care?

About the Authors

Augusta Moore is currently experiencing her 973rd reincarnated form, having moved up from her last incarnation as an arctic krill, and is hoping to get it right this time. She's not sure writing this book has helped.

Elizabeth Ripley has spent her life devoted to world peace, and hopes that through this book, her dream of a world summit including Louis Farrakhan, the Pope, the spirits of Baha Ullah, and L. Ron Hubbard may finally be realized.